Also in this Series

Steam Coasters & Short Sea Traders *3rd Edition, 1994*
by C.V.Waine & R.S.Fenton *ISBN 0905184 15 7.   182 pages.*
The history of the British steam coaster covering, building, repairing, early design, Clyde Puffers and the various engines-aft types, up to the big east coast colliers. Also covered are those with engines amidships and coastal tankers. This new edition has a much expanded text with 25 extra pages concentrating on the smaller coasting shipowners, as owners mainly in the coal trade on the east coast and Irish Sea are now covered in a companion volume, *The Steam Collier Fleets*. Illustrated with 76 plans and 29 colour profiles selected with the modelmaker in mind plus 97 black and white sketches and photos.

British Ocean Tramps. Volume 1. Builders & Cargoes.
by P.N.Thomas   *ISBN 0 905184 13 0.   158 pages.*
A major study of the ships which were the backbone of British commerce, this first volume defines the tramp steamer and looks at construction and builders, including short histories of the main builders. The different designs are fully illustrated including those for world war one and two. The cargoes, coal, grain, ore, timber etc, and how they were carried. Shipbroking: how the ships got their cargoes; chartering, freight rates and unseaworthiness. Steam tramps in world events, particularly in wars great and small. With 48 detailed plans and colour plates, 54 photos, maps and diagrams.

British Ocean Tramps. Volume 2. Owners & Their Ships.
by P.N.Thomas. *ISBN 0905184 14 9. 182 pages.*
The second volume in a major study of the ships which were the backbone of British commerce. Owners and Crews. Histories of the major and minor owners, some 1,300 companies in all, including the early companies active in the 19th century. Notes on some 2,400 ships and typical voyage patterns. Characteristic naming patterns used by the companies. Illustrated with 56 photos from the 1890s to the 1950s, 22 colour profiles and 34 plans.

British Steam Tugs
by P.N.Thomas.   *ISBN 0 905184 07 6.   222 pages.*
*This book is beautifully produced and a must for anyone at all interested in these fascinating craft..*MODEL BOATS. A full history covering early tugs, wood iron and steel paddle tugs; harbour, seeking and coastal screw tugs, and ocean tugs. Thames craft tugs, tenders and passenger carrying tugs, naval and wartime tugs. Tug owners and builders. Tug construction, engines and deck gear. Over 1000 steam tugs, 100 builders and 400 owners are covered. The tug plans range from 1833 to 1956, and 29 colour profiles will be of interest to modellers. More than 90 photographs (some colour), sketches, and colour diagram of 88 funnel colours.

The Steam Collier Fleets
by J.A.MacRae & C.V.Waine.   *ISBN 0 905184 12 2.   226 pages.*
This book was begun by Captain Jim MacRae aboard the Thames up-river collier HACKNEY and with Dr. Charles Waine produced this companion volume to **Steam Coasters & Short Sea Traders**. *A book to delight the coaster enthusiast, model-maker or just about anyone who likes pictures of ships...The result must surely deserve the accolade of a definitive work, something which will be referred to time and again...*SEA BREEZES. A full history of the colliers and coasters in the coal trade of the British Isles and near Continent covering over 800 owners, 1200 ships and the harbours built to serve them. Illustrated with 93 ship plans and coloured profiles, 55 photos, some in colour and 53 sketches, harbour maps and charts.

Old Time Steam Coasting
by O.G.Spargo & T.H.Thomason.   *ISBN 0 905184 07 6.   138 pages.*
An eye witness acount of life in Liverpool steam coasters in the 1920s and 1930s. *Between them the authors have made a tremendous contribution to the field of both maritime and social history, for their sharp and detailed accounts provide us with a wealth of important information of the kind which is far too often omitted from shipping histories...*SHIPS MONTHLY. The operation of the coasting trade, vessels, crews and cargoes are fully described. Six colour plates, 5 plans and numerous sketches, photos and voyage charts.

Estuary & River Ferries of South West England
by Martin Langley & Edwina Small.   *ISBN 0 905184 08 4.   148 pages.*
The many creeks and rivers of the area had rowing and sailing ferries which were later replaced by paddle and screw steamers or steam chain ferries in a number of cases. Full histories of some 139 ferries and over 300 boats are supported by sketch maps, plans (some in colour), and photographs from the River Severn in the north around the coast to the River Stour, Christchurch and Poole in the south.

The Wandering Worfe
by D.H.Robinson.   *ISBN 0 905184 06 8.   130 pages.*
An environmental and historical study of an **east Shropshire** river and its tributary streams, which flows into the River Severn near Bridgnorth. It describes the water and other mills and the uses to which they were put, reservoirs and other water sources and their place in local history. Two coloured maps and 89 black and white photos, maps, sketches and plans.

1. *Around 1760 J.June published a pattern book for ship decorators with sketches of figureheads, taffrails, quarters, etc. These are a few of his sketches. They show the figureheads sitting astride the stem timber in the peculiar posture dictated by the curve of the bow.*
(Courtesy John Watson)

2. *Very few pictures of ship carvers exist. This rare photograph shows Arthur Levison of Gloucester posing beside a typical "owner's wife" figurehead which he has just completed. When asked to date this photograph the Manchester Museum of Costume commented that the clothing was pseudo-classical and could not be dated in any way. (Richard Hunter collection)*

BRITISH FIGUREHEAD & SHIP CARVERS

P. N. Thomas

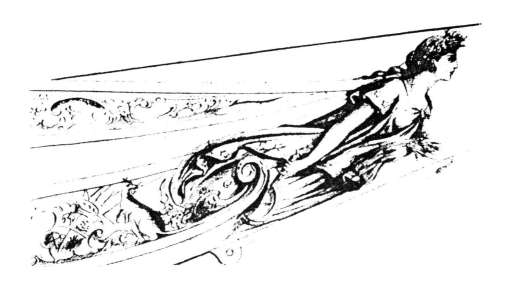

3. *This typical figurehead of Ceres comes from a note book belonging to the shipbuilder Robert Napier and almost certainly was intended for the steamship* Australasian *3662/84. The details on the trail board match those on the rigging plan. (Courtesy Transport Museum, Glasgow)*

Illustrated by Richard Hunter.

WAINE Research

Publications

This book is dedicated to John H. Burlinson of Miami, Florida who encouraged me all those years ago to take up 'figurehead hunting' as a hobby.

4. Derry Castle 1367/83 *was the last sailing ship launched by Dobie & Co. of Glasgow. She had a short career being wrecked in New Zealand in 1887. The members of the crew who perished were buried on the shore surrounded by pieces of the wreck, watched over by the figurehead which was probably the work of M. & J. Allan.*

By the same author: British Steam Tugs.
British Ocean Tramps.

Published by:
Waine Research,
Mount Pleasant,
Beamish Lane,
Albrighton,
Wolverhampton,
England. WV7 3JJ.

First published 1995

Printed and bound in England.

Contents

Dimensions of Figureheads and Lacing Pieces.

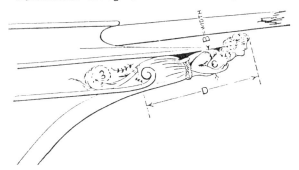

Simpson's Naval Constructor published in 1904 provided tables for all manner of ship fittings. Mr. Simpson even saw fit to advise shipbuilders as to the size of the figurehead.

A LENGTH OF VESSEL, B. S.	B SIZE OF LACING PIECE.	C DEPTH OF FIGURE-HEAD.	D LENGTH OF FIGURE OUTSIDE OF STEM.	
Feet.	Inches.	Inches.	Feet.	Inches.
450	12¼	30¼	9	6
400	12	28½	9	0
350	11¼	26¾	8	6
300	10½	25	8	0
250	9¾	23¼	7	6
200	9	21½	7	0
150	8¼	19¾	6	6
100	7½	18	6	0
NOTE.—Angle of lacing piece, 45°.				

N.B. Photographs and sketches are indicated thus-( ). Merchant ships are identified by gross tonnage and the last two digits of date of build. Dates are in the 1800's unless otherwise specified. Naval vessels are identified by 'rate', number of guns and year of build except for those built in the latter years of the 19th. century, where the displacement tonnage is used. Occasionally tonnage is given as 'b.m.', which is builder's measure, or 't.m.', which is Thames measurement. Quotations from old Naval documents are reproduced with the original spelling.

6. Port Stanley 2187/90 *at the Ballast Bank at Troon, Ayrshire. She was one of John Roberts' "stock" figureheads for which he charged only £3.15.0. Although attractively carved the price is reflected in the simplistic detailing where a single chisel stroke is used to make a fold. In many of Roberts' figureheads the index finger of the hand holding the robe is shown extended.*

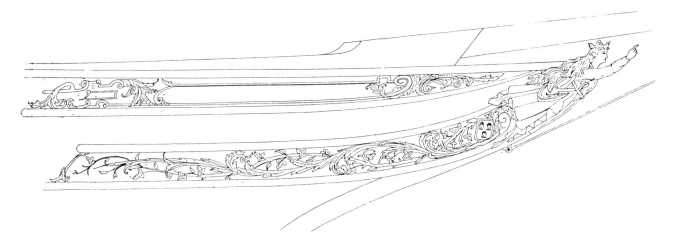

Foreword

7. St.Sunniva 1368/31 *was built by Hall, Russell of Aberdeen, the last commercial steamship to have a clipper bow and a figurehead, a feature which the newspapers hardly saw fit to mention. The outstretched arm was removed to avoid damage in heavy weather.* *(Aberdeen Maritime Museum)*

About thirty years ago I was walking along the Ballast Bank at Troon in Ayrshire. There was a row of cottages beside the path, protected from the wind and waves by a wall, and visible through an open door a figurehead was on display in a courtyard. I had no particular interest in figureheads but had never seen one close to before and in any case, being a ship lover, a photograph of her was a 'must'. She was *Port Stanley 2187/90*, built by Russell of Port Glasgow and broken up in Troon in 1924. (The yard records show that she had been carved by John Roberts of Port Glasgow). Some time later a letter appeared in a magazine from an American named John Burlinson asking for photographs of figureheads, and I sent him a print of *Port Stanley*. He was delighted to receive a picture of a 'new' figurehead and asked if I had any more, which I had not. However, asking around the office the ex-Navy boys told me about Rosyth and Govan, (in Glasgow), enabling me to add five more to my score. When the family went on holiday to Whitby I made enquiries and kept my eyes open adding another nine to my bag. Anyone going on holiday from the office was cajoled into helping and another dozen 'new' figureheads were discovered. Pictures of all these were sent to John Burlinson and after five years a quick check showed that I had quite a number of negatives of figureheads and so, out of curiousity, these were printed off and a love affair with figureheads began. As is usual with me, the very fact that at that time so little was available about them and little interest seemed to be displayed impelled me to start researching the subject. Over the years between us John and I raised his total of 350 figureheads preserved in Britain to over 500. However, many of these have since been sold abroad, decayed beyond redemption, or simply disappeared. Over the years I have exchanged photographs with many people with whom I have since lost touch; if any of them read this book- "Hello there."

Every book and article on figureheads said the same thing. "Very little is known about the men who carved them." So I decided to do something about this vacuum. Nothing could be easier, just look up the launch reports in the newspapers and note the name of the carver. As it turned out it was not easy to find the launch reports, difficult to make them out on the microfilm reader, and more to the point, most reports did not mention the figurehead let alone the carver. Then I remembered a comment which I had heard on the radio that in Victorian times a newspaper gave its readers 'news', not what was happening locally as everyone knew that already, they wanted to know what was going on elsewhere in the country or the world. In any case, every ship had a figurehead so that was not news. To the reporter a launch was a social event and what mattered was which dignitaries were there, what they said, and who the lady was who christened the ship. Many times you were left in ignorance as to the type of ship which had just gone down the slips. The most satisfactory source of information was the few shipyard records which have survived, but even then there were disappointments with complete hull costs without a single supplier's name. Worse still there was one case where there was a supplier's name against every item until it came to the figurehead where it merely said "To carver £6."

As far as possible I have used photographs which have not previously been published, and have concentrated on using those where the carver is known. The main collections of information have been in Glasgow, Aberdeen and Newcastle. In many other parts of the country I drew a complete blank except for the directory entries.

My thanks go to the archivists who have helped me in my search and to those 'unknowns' who had to descend into the lower regions to bring up those heavy tomes to satisfy my insatiable demands. Also to those institutions which have given me permission to use their material and to reproduce drawings, photographs and sketches. The National Maritime Museum, Public Record Office, Victoria & Albert Museum, Strathclyde Regional Archives, Glasgow University Business Records and the Alexander Turnbull Library, New Zealand. The Public Record Office holds the old Admiralty records and without these it would have been impossible to write about the naval carvers. They have allowed me to copy much original material which is Crown Copyright and some of this is reproduced by permission of the Controller of Her Majesty's Stationery Office. Unfortunately there was a clear-out of material from 1861 onwards which leaves us still in ignorance about the final years of the naval figurehead carver. Thanks to the Admiralty as well for allowing me to use photographs which I took years ago in a 'sweep' round the dockyards. I must not forget Richard Hunter, another enthusiast, who has helped to find suitable illustrations and has drawn sketches where the original photographs were not suitable for reproduction.

The art of the ship carver is not extinct. There are still men today working at the trade. Jack Whitehead who cut a new figurehead for *Falls of Clyde 1809/79,* and with Norman Gaiches carved *Warrior.* Trevor Ellis who cut a new figurehead for *Unicorn.* Greg Powlesland whose carving graces the bows of *Balclutha 1716/86.*

In the Spring 1991 Mariners' Museum Journal there was an article entitled 'Figurehead Carvers; their artistry and craftsmanship.' Those two words sum it all up for me -'artistry and craftsmanship.'

8. London 249/25 *is a small figurehead which was on the bows of an early steamship. It shows the style affected by some carvers to reproduce the appearance of a classical stone bust. (Hull Maritime Museum.)*

8. *In contrast to* London, Countess of Galloway 145/35, *another small figurehead, also from a steamer, has a style which, though lifelike, some would call naive.* *(Kirkcudbright Museum)*

9. *The "Saracen" or the "Man with the Turban" on the wall of a house in the Royal Mile in Edinburgh.*

9. *This house in London was built in 1716 and the unknown figurehead is reputed to have been erected on its wall a few years later.*

1. Merchant Ship Figureheads

When the subject of ships' figureheads is raised, two questions are immediately asked; 'when and why?' 'When' can be traced back to prehistoric times when the caveman scratched pictures on the rocks or drew on the walls of his cave with the end of a burnt stick. Most of these primitive representations of boats have at one end what students identify as animal heads.'Why' is a matter of conjecture and several explanations have been advanced. Was it some form of tribal identification, some form of idol, or was it an image to frighten the enemy? My own feeling is that when early man took to the water he soon found that his life was threatened by wind and wave and none but an unfriendly god could have caused his troubles. To placate this god he had to make a blood sacrifice and to prove that this had indeed been made he mounted the head on one end of his frail craft. Over the years the figurehead did take on a religious aspect. The Romans used a human form on their galleys, as did the Greeks, while the Egyptians used an image of an animal or bird. By the Middle Ages men were using sail and on the bow of the medieval cog was a small 'beak', just large enough to carry the effigy of an animal. None of these have survived and we have to rely on seals and coats of arms as evidence.

The earliest example of the merchant ship figurehead which has been preserved is *Golden Cherubs* to be found aboard *Cutty Sark*, a small double figure which has been attributed to Grinling Gibbons, the famous wood carver, as it contains features which he favoured when carving. The vessel which bore it was a smuggling ship built in about 1660 and she was wrecked at Tintagel in 1703. There was a much weathered figure on the walls of the Smugglers' Cafe in Whitby, about 3 feet in height and with an upright stance. In Edinburgh on a building in the Royal Mile is a small stone carving which local legend says is based on a figurehead of a vessel of the 17th century. There is a story behind the 'man with the turban' (9). About 350 years ago a young Edinburgh man was to be hung for robbery but he escaped in a ship which was later captured by pirates. He was sold as a slave but gained favour with the Sultan who bought him. Set free in 1645 he sailed for Edinburgh to sack the city but when he arrived he found it in the grip of a plague which he knew how to cure. He relented and helped to save the people. The city pardoned him and invited him to stay but he would not dwell within the city walls. He built a house outside its boundary and on its wall mounted a replica of the figurehead of his ship.

Roger Finch's books on pier-head painters frequently portray small vessels and show that those built before 1830 usually had almost vertical stems with little or no decoration. There were exceptions of course. In common with many American and Canadian built vessels the whaler *Truelove 296/1774* had a 'beak' with carvings extending down the stem. The Isle of Man brig *Caesar* of 1783 had a scroll forming a fiddlehead, while *Crown 297/21* had a billethead, carved by John Askew. Larger ships had figureheads; *Christian 459/18* and *John* of 1811, (belonging to Wells) each had a small bust set upright on an extended stem. Some had full length figureheads on the bow frequently standing on a bracket on the stempiece with one foot before the other. When Scott's of Greenock wrote to Archibald Robertson of Liverpool they suggested that the figurehead of *John Scott 305/29* should be " a striding or stepping off figure". The old East Indiamen were designed on warship lines and generally had naval type figureheads. A picture of a stranded East Indiaman painted in 1821 showed a vessel like a warship with an extended stem with headrails and a 'split' figure in armour astride the bow, a style often used on large naval vessels of the 18th. century. Before the second world war there were two figureheads from this era still extant, one a small female figure about 4 feet high with an upright posture and the other a life-size figure depicting Queen Elizabeth (80).

Fortunately there is one source of information which gives a very clear picture of the figurehead at the end of the 18th century. The artist William Anderson spent much of his time in the shipyards of the Thames and one of his sketch books covering the period 1792 to 1794 has survived. In this he recorded in detail and sometimes in colour the figureheads and stern galleries of ships on the stocks (11). Some vessels had full sets of head rails like a warship with an upright figure while another, *Trinity Yacht 141/1795* had an old fashioned beak with a lion standing thereon.

As the 19th century progressed it became more or less mandatory that a British ship should have a figurehead or a simple bow decoration of some kind. About this time Peter Hedderwick published his book on Naval Architecture and in it he wrote the following definitions:
"1.The Figurehead is one which is the figure of a man, woman or the like.

2.The Billet-head or scroll-head is one finished off with two scrolls or volutes turning outwards.

3.The Fiddle-head is finished off with only one scroll or volute having the spiral turning inwards towards the vessel.

The Figurehead is most in vogue, almost all vessels of considerable size have them. The Billet-head is more admired than the Fiddle-head. On vessels between 100 and 300 tons the projection of the head should be about 1/13th. of the ship's length. Small vessels have commonly busts or half figures as these have a better effect than full figures."

The subject for the figurehead was predominantly female despite the sailors' superstition that a woman aboard ship would bring bad luck. She might be the owner's wife or daughter. She might be a figure from classical literature, a goddess perhaps. All too frequently she was "anonymous", merely a female form dressed in flowing robes. One feature which was very common was that one hand should be crossed across the breast holding a flower as a symbol of purity. This was not always so, as other objects might be placed in her grasp. At Southwold there is the figure of a young girl in Victorian costume holding a bunch of grapes, indicating a connection with the wine or fruit trade. At one time on the Isle of Mull a small figurehead from *Kate 73/62* was to be found holding a fish in her hand. She came from a fish carrier and her arm was mobile and would be positioned to show how good had been the catch, upheld for a good catch, down for a poor haul. In Great Yarmouth *Patricia* ex *Miranda 793/1909* (13) held in her hand two doves. *Calliope* the muse of poetry is shown with a clay tablet in her grasp. The commonest is *Ceres* holding the Horn of Plenty, a cornucopia,or a sheaf of wheat. Many figureheads have survived of *Ceres* but no details have survived with them and in many cases the name of the vessel was not in fact *Ceres*. The figurehead of Napier's *Australasian 3662/84* clearly shows the sheaf of wheat below her arm (3). Ships were often christened after well known personalities and the carver would portray them faithfully as he

11. *William Anderson portrayed* Eling Grove *with a Scot in full highland dress holding a long bow in his hand. There is a mystery here as Eling is a village near Southampton and the long bow was not much used by the Scots. As can be seen the bow of a small East Indiaman was the same as that of the warships of the period. (Victoria and Albert Museum)*

worked. *William Wilberforce 172/16*, aboard the *Cutty Sark*. The ill-fated Mary Stuart appeared on the bows of the steam yacht *Queen of Scots 603/04*. One rather odd figurehead was that of a witch on a broomstick, wearing a typical Welsh hat, located at one time at Torpoint.

Male figures were less common. Frequently the shipowner would present himself as the subject for the figurehead. Famous men or politicians in frock coats holding a scroll were another source of inspiration. Such a figurehead was from *Earl of Mar and Kellie 430/56* and was found under a pile of hay on a Scottish farm. At one time in Whitby a figure representing Sir Robert Napier stood decaying in a back garden hidden from the public gaze. Normally the carver could be relied on to produce a good likeness of the personality after whom the vessel was named. Gods and legendary figures abounded. Of *Neptune*'s there are plenty but few with any history. Hall of Aberdeen built *Robin Hood 852/56* with a half length figure of the famous outlaw carrying his bow in his hand. This figurehead was an oddity as the vessel had an upright bow and a knee had to be affixed to it to support the figure. Even the common working man found his place on the bows of the steamer *Wearmouth 594/55* whose figurehead, carved by James Brooker of Sunderland, depicted a miner with his pick, lamp and canteen, named after a colliery in token of her connection with the coal trade. Occasionally a sailor might appear. In Shoreham there is a replica of a figurehead which rotted away, which depicts a sailor of the early years dressed in a smock. A small figurehead of a sailor in uniform had *Undaunted* painted on his straw hat. The Highlander was another favourite and there are numerous unknown kilted warriors in museums all over the world. Many portrayed the Scot as a belligerent character with a claymore raised to strike an unknown enemy. Animals were a rarity. *Sirius 180/37*, the first steamer to cross the Atlantic under steam alone had as her figurehead a dog to represent the Dog Star and this has survived and is preserved in the museum at Hull. In the collection at Tresco they have a lion, a salmon and an eagle. *Lowestoft 294/66* (28) carried below her bowsprit a grotesque representation of a fish which can still be seen in the Life-Saving house at Tynemouth. Even more grotesque was a figurehead in a photograph of an unknown vessel with the head and fore body of a lion and the wings and tail of a dragon. Any vessel called *Pegasus* was liable to have a flying horse figurehead. Corsar of Liverpool put a horse on all their vessels, not only on their *Pegasus 2564/84*. Further down the scale came the billet-head, generally cheaper than a figurehead, though John Roberts of Greenock charged the same for both. The very least that could be done was to have scrollwork carved on the trailboards, or, as was done on *Wave Queen* of 1861, which had none, the stem was carved and the design was carried right down to the waterline. Could it be that the twirls of the scroll represented the curly fleece of a sacrificed sheep? A more elaborate decoration appeared on the trailboards of *Latimer 1649/85* ,which had, surrounded by ornamental scrolls, an open book which read "Hear instruction, be wise and refuse it not. "The tea clipper *Chaa*

Sze 556/60, (41), which means tea taster, had her trailboards embellished with the figure of a Chinaman, tea bushes, chests of tea and tea cups.

Double figureheads had been found on the 'Old Wooden Walls' but these were a rarity on merchant ships. However *Partenope 1646/75* built by Evans of Liverpool had two female figures, one either side of the bow. *Salamis 1130/75,* built in Aberdeen had a billethead with a small Grecian warrior on each side. Tod & McGregor launched *Faid Rabani 600/52,* a steam yacht for Egypt, and on her bow was the crest of the Pasha of Egypt supported by two lions. Seath of Rutherglen built *Alma 95/54* with a multiple figurehead comprising a soldier of the 93rd. Highlanders charging with bayonet fixed, supported on either side by a French and a Turkish soldier.

Usually the figureheads of deep-sea ships were painted white, thereby avoiding any accusation of idolatry or superstition -"not a true likeness of anything in the heavens or on the earth or the waters beneath the earth." Small merchant ships and naval vessels usually had their figureheads painted in lifelike colours. From time to time a puzzle arises where the figurehead does not appear to suit the name. Denny's *Jason 1023/57* was given a female figurehead at the request of her owner who had been captain of a ship called *Jason* many years before. Maybe it was superstition or maybe she represented one of the two women in Jason's life, Atalanta and Medea. *Greta 1190/74* bore on her bow the likeness of Robert Southey, the poet, Greta being the name of a river in Cumberland whence Southey came (22). The figurehead of *Lady Lilford* 126/42 was that of a midshipman but the family can offer no explanation for this.

How do you carve a figurehead? None of the old books on wood carving in the reference library even mentioned figureheads, though I recall reading in a fairly modern one a remark which put the figurehead carvers at the bottom of the league table as far as wood carving was concerned, accusing them of being heavy-handed and failing to grasp the finer points of wood carving. I disagree totally with that comment and never cease to admire their craftsmanship, though there was a 'league table' among the ship carvers themselves from the true artist who specialised in the cutting of figureheads to the anonymous craftsman in the small shipyard who chiselled out a naive but passable representation of the human form. In the Harper's Weekly of 5th. March 1892 their reporter Will M. Clemens had a chat with an old carver and he wrote an article in this vein:

"I tarried awhile by the table of the figurehead carver and watched his shining blades make their keen never-erring strokes. I looked with curious interest on the huge shapeless block of wood out of which he was cutting a naiad to adorn the prow of a big ship. The workplace of the ship

12. (Left). Pelican 97/38 *was one of the few vessels to carry a bird on her bow. (Hastings Museum).*

12. (Below). *This picture shows the bow carving of* Kathleen & May 136/00 *which represents the minimum decoration which was expected on a coasting schooner. (Craig/Farr collection).*

13. Derry Castle 1367/83 *is shown here in close-up where she stood guard over her dead sailors on an island off Auckland. It is not known if this magnificent figurehead by M. & J. Allan has been preserved.*

13. *The steam yacht* Patricia 793/09 *was used as a tender by Trinity House. She had been built as* Miranda *at Southampton and probably represents the heroine of Shakespeare's Tempest.*

carver was for all the world like an old curiosity shop. When I asked what were the preliminaries of the work he told me that the first thing to be considered was the shape of the ship's bow and the rake of the bowsprit. On their proportions depended the size of the figure. The original design was drawn on paper with crayons which in its rough state gave only the slightest suggestion of the finished work. A solid block was chosen, the average length of a figurehead being seven to eight feet. The block was roughed out on the floor and then lifted on to 'horses' where it was finished. The only tools were chisels, mallets, gouges and sandpaper. Once he had started on the figure the paper design was of little use and he had to depend almost entirely on his eye to get the expression and the proportions right. As with everything else the amount of labour expended depended upon the price. Some figures could be finished in a few weeks and others required months for completion." He told Clemens that it was no easy task to carve a figurehead as he had many things to contend with especially the eccentricities of the owners or skippers.

It seems to me that this description is over-simplified and that there was much more than this to the carving of a figurehead. First there is the 'mould'. Moulds for figureheads are often mentioned in correspondence but so far no description has been found. In 1789 Mr. Brockbank of Lancaster included "head moulds" in his inventory. In 1826 the Stephen's yard in Arbroath thanked the Aberdeen yard for sending down a figurehead and for returning its mould, while they in turn advised that a mould for the stern of a ship in their yard was on its way up by sea. The naval shipyard at Woolwich reported that the mould for the block for the figurehead of *H.M.S. Imperieuse 2358 b.m./52* was ready in the mould loft, but that they had no yellow pine in stock with which to prepare the block. In 1890 Charles Connell was asking Kay & Reid, the carvers, to return the mould with the completed figurehead for their No.174, *Othomarschen 1787/91*. In addition to all this we have the words of Peter Hedderwick in his book on Naval Architecture: "The head should first be drawn on the plan of the vessel and then laid down on the floor of the mould loft, and moulds made to the same." As the 'mould loft' is mentioned it is safe to assume that the mould was made of the same thin wood sections which were used to make moulds for the ships' frames, and that it would define the area between the stem of the vessel and the bowsprit. When the block was being prepared, as well as being checked against the mould, the carver's sketch would be needed to ensure that the block was the right shape without wasting valuable yellow pine. The block for a large figurehead had to be "fitted", that is, made up to size with several slabs of timber, dowelled and glued together. In 1854 Woolwich Dockyard was looking for yellow pine at least 18" thick to make up a block. The whole procedure was quite complicated and quite a bit of money had to be spent before the figurehead was even paid for. An old shipwright's notebook in the National Maritime Museum gives us an idea of the procedure and the costs.

Prices in H. M. Dockyards in 1857.

Making mould:

Whole length	Make mould for, trim and put together		9/6
	Get into place and bolt.		£4. 8. 0
	Unbolt, clear and take down		£2. 2. 0
Bust	Make mould for, trim and put together		8/6
	Get into place and bolt		£1. 2. 0
	Unbolt, clear and take down.		18/0

To make block for figure:

Above 1800 tons	5/6
900-1800 tons	4/6
below 900 tons.	3/6

An entry in Mr.Brockbank's yard book in 1798 throws further light on the procedure for fitting a figurehead:

April 1798. W. Mulvey, Thos. Bland and Richard Proctor, apprentice, agree:

To fit the head of *Union*	£10.0.0.
Raise the bowsprit hook	1.1.0.
Prepare the moulds	19/0.

14. *Passed down through the family this little figure was always called* Lady Lilford 126/42. *The puzzle is why a naval officer should represent a female name.*

14. *This figurehead is believed to have come from the schooner* Greenhithe 162/74. *The Manchester Museum of Costume were impressed with the accuracy with which the carver had followed the fashion of the period.*

What about the wood from which the carved work was cut? For a long time elm was used but it had the disadvantage that with constant wetting it became soft and rotted. When *H.M.S. Prince Royal 1187 b.m./10* was re-built in 1640 twenty loads of elm were used. Much of the secondary carved work on these early warships was cut from the pine of old masts and spars. The stern carving of *Royal Charles 1230 b.m./55*, captured by the Dutch in 1667, is on display in a Dutch museum and this use of old timber can readily be seen. With the weight of the carved work on the stem, vessels tended to pitch heavily in rough seas and indeed, in 1710, the Admiralty reported a complaint from the captain of *Essex 1090 b.m./79* in this respect. Around 1700 oak was used for carved work, while at the same time the Admiralty ordered a reduction in the decorative work which would improve the seaworthiness of the ships. In 1737 they also instructed the dockyards to use lighter and more durable timber for figureheads and trailboards. The records of Charles Hill around 1800 show that they used elm and later oak for figureheads and deal for the arms. The cost seems to have been about 1/7 per cubic foot. The letters in the Admiralty collection which start in 1830 confirm that by that by that time yellow pine was the timber which they issued to the carver.

The cost books of H S. Edwards of North Shields indicate that they used American Fir (which may have been yellow pine) costing 1/8 per cubic foot, except on their *Castle Green* of 1839 where they used mahogany. The Connell of Glasgow cost books of 1884 indicate that two grades of yellow pine were being used. For the body of the figurehead they used expensive wood at 3/3 per cubic foot, while for the arms they bought wood costing only 10¾d per cubic foot. They usually inserted a segment of elm in the back of the figurehead. When the new owner of *Derwent* 1970/84 went to McMillan of Dumbarton for his ship he wanted the figurehead to last and had it carved in teak. The 12 foot high lion figurehead has survived and now, over 100 years old, is on display in the Mariners' Museum, Newport News. Another shipowner was even more determined that one of his figureheads should resist wind and weather. *C.E.Spooner 160/78* carried on her bow a copper bust of her namesake, the engineer who worked on the Festiniog railway.

A passing thought about that block! According to the Connell cost books they usually sent the carver a block of yellow pine of 30 to 35 cubic feet. At 38 pounds per cubic foot the block would then weigh between 1140 and 1330 pounds. Assuming a wastage of 50% during the carving process a figurehead for the average 'clipper' would weigh from 570 to 665 pounds, (260 to 300 kg). This had then to be transported by horse and cart, handled into place, supported and secured. Quite a job! In the chapter on Naval carvings the point is raised about protective ironwork being erected around the carved work. In a brief specification for *Min-y-Don 1149/75* by A. & J. Inglis of Pointhouse, Glasgow dated 1875 we read: "To have neat ¾ figure with necessary carved work on stern, head boards and gangway boards. Head and stern to be protected with galvanised iron bars."

15. *In concentrating on figureheads it is all too easy to forget that this was only one part of the carver's task. He also carved stern boards such as that of the* City of Bristol *539/50 built on the Wear and lost off the Tyne in 1870. The carving is now preserved in the Tynemouth Life Brigade House.*

Who designed the figureheads? Sometimes the carver, sometimes the shipbuilder or the owner. From time to time we find another party involved when the naval authorities went to an eminent sculptor who would provide a suitable bust to ensure that the features of a famous person would be accurately portrayed. In 1877 Herr Emil Steiner approached the Admiralty requesting permission to make models for figureheads for English ships to which they replied: "No. This work is entrusted to English artists." A book called "In Memoriam" published in Aberdeen in 1898 tells us that "George Russell, the well-known sculptor, began his artistic career designing figureheads." In the mid 1700's J. June, (sculp.) published a small pamphlet or booklet entitled "*A new Book of Ornaments for the use of all who are any way conversant in designing, Building, Carving, Painting and Drawing Ships*". In this he offered a selection of patterns for decorative carving for ship bows and sterns.

It would be unfair to pass judgement on many of the figureheads whose photographs appear in this book when one considers that most of them are over 100 years old and there is no way of knowing how much restoration has been carried out or how many coats of paint have 'blunted' the sharpness of the detail. Frequently, however, there is no doubt about the ability of the carver. It is a pity that due to lack of historical evidence only a few of their carvers have been identified. To many early collectors the important thing was the attractiveness of the figurehead and its provenance was of less significance. Over the years memories have become less sharp and the source of a figurehead has been forgotten. Outside a cafe in Runswick Bay there sat two figureheads, a Neptune and a female bust. "Oh! We call her Amelia." they said. It so happens that a brig named *Amelia 237/33* was wrecked in Runswick Bay in 1857 but is this enough for a positive identification?

As noted earlier there was the possibility that a figurehead may have represented a god. Believe it or not, according to a Dundee newspaper, there was a figurehead which became a goddess. W. B. Thompson of Dundee launched *Juteopolis* 2842/91 and many years later under her new name of *Garthpool* she went aground and was wrecked. The figurehead was washed ashore at Boavista and was regarded as divine by the natives who worshipped it every day. The owner of *Garthpool,* Sir William Garthwaite visited the island and bought the 'goddess' from them for £50. It is probable that the figurehead had been carved by James Law the well-known Dundee carver.

With all this talk of figureheads we are prone to forget that the work of the ship carver did not end when one was fitted on the stem of the vessel. On the early sailing ships and on the better class ones of later years a good pair of trailboards was essential so that the figurehead blended in sweetly with the sheer of the rail. On the later cheaply built ships trailboards were omitted, thereby saving £2 or £3 but having the result that the figurehead seemed to be just stuck on to the stem, conforming to convention, but with a look of not belonging. Sterns were also important, even on the older steamships. At one time the ship carver used the stern as an artist used a canvas, portraying characters conjured up by the name of the vessel (15), but as the years passed the pictorial aspect was abandoned and typically there would simply be bands of carved rope meeting at a badge, shield, or star at the centre of the stern(65). Paddle steamers gave the carver something to work on even when the straight stem precluded the fitting of a figurehead. There were many magnificent medallions to be seen at the centre of the "ray" of the paddle box slots (107). Elsewhere other outlets were available for the carver in decorating columns, panelling, skylights, steering gear covers, and also very important, the big mirror in the main saloon. This latter featured in every Connell enquiry even after all other forms of secondary carving had been given up. The concentration on the decorative aspect of the figurehead has overshadowed other forms of ship carving with the result that few examples of the ship carvers' other work have survived, save for the many name boards off wrecked ships which adorn the walls of lifeboat stations all around our coasts.

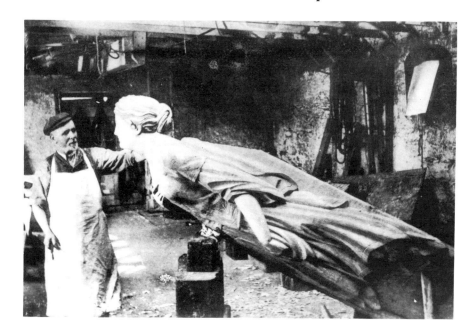

2. Merchant Ship Carvers

Albert Works Co.   This name occurs late-on in a couple of shipyard records but so far the location of the firm remains a mystery. In 1898 Lobnitz & Co. of Renfrew paid a bill for £101.11.6, probably for two steam yachts which they had just completed, *Vacuna 47 t.m./98* and *Xanthus 122/98*, a change from the dredgers for which they were famed. In 1897 they received from Alexander Stephen of Linthouse, two equal payments of £42.13.4 for the steamers *Alexandria 6917/97* and *Boadicea 7057/98*, while in 1903 they cut the internal carved work for *Hellig Olav 10072/03*. Stephens paid them £130.0.0 for carved work and inlays for *Miltiades 6765/03*, a clipper-bowed passenger liner with a rather magnificent figurehead.

M. & J. Allan, Glasgow.   M. & J. Allan of Glasgow appear in the Trades Directory from about 1839, at first as Mitchell and John Allan and later as Mitchell and James Allan. Over the years the firm expanded until by 1861 they were employing 5 men and 5 boys while by 1871 they had 20 men and boys in their workshop. In 1881 their staff had fallen to 7 men and 3 boys. In the census records James is described as a "wood carver" while Mitchell is called a "master wood carver and turner." Both men originated in Edinburgh. The brothers worked for a number of shipyards. In 1852 they cut for Denny of Dumbarton a figurehead for *Rhoderick Dhu 376/53* which portrayed the hero of Sir Walter Scott's epic poem, one of the many figureheads depicting a Highlander. Scott's of Greenock gave them orders between 1869 and 1895 for carvings for 40 sailing ships, steamers and steam yachts. Their first contract for Scott's was the complete carved work for *Christian McCausland 962/69* costing £51.19.6 and *Jessie Readman 962/69* which cost £54.19.6.

Figurehead, name, and trail boards and stern ornaments.

24 saloon trusses, gilded.

4 corner trusses, gilded.

4 capitals for lobby, of teak.

6 half capitals--do--

One mirror and carved frame complete.

2 half trusses---do---

54 deckhouse trusses of teak.

Their performance on these first contracts was not impressive as they completely failed to meet the required delivery date and the shipyard had to press hard to have the figureheads finished in time for the launches. The figureheads and the trailboards had to be fitted before the vessels were launched or the launch could be delayed by up to two weeks. They received some orders for very expensively decorated ships. *Ajaccio 1209/72* brought them in £357.10.6. *Gogo 648/72* in the same year was worth £119.4.0 and *Hekla 3528/84* came to £89.18.2. Between 1868 and 1872 they executed carved work for some vessels for Charles Connell though only one, *County of Lanark 498/68* was specifically named and her cost was £23.8.9. J. & G. Thompson of Clydebank went to them during the period 1859 to 1892 but the entries in the cash books do not give the names of the ships for which the carved work was intended. (40). Only two names were recorded, *Giraffe 677/60* which brought them £19.13.0. and *Emerald Isle 784/62* on which £14.0.0 was spent. They also did a small job for the yard of Alexander Stephen in Govan in 1850 but again the cash book gives no names.

In the cost books for Robert Duncan of Port Glasgow between 1864 and 1894 the name Allan appears against no fewer than 81 vessels (19). Some of these were cut in the Glasgow workshop while others were by the hand of James Allan, junior, either working on his own or on behalf of his uncles. M. & J. Allan must have built up a reputation for fine carvings as they received orders from other shipbuilding centres. For Alexander Hall of Aberdeen they cut figureheads and carved work for *Calypso 1061/74* for £60.9.0 and *Port Jackson 2212/82* for £31.9.0. When Richardson Bros. of Stockton required a figurehead for the clipper-bowed steamer *Sir Colin Campbell 600/55* they called on M. & J. Allan to carve a likeness of the military hero of that name.

There were dozens of small shipyards on the Clyde and M. & J. Allan provided carved work for several of these. They were somewhat unfortunate in their choice of customer as many of them went bankrupt. In 1864 The Clyde Shipbuilding & Engineering Company of Port Glasgow 'went to the wall' owing money to M. & J. Allan. One of the directors, Henry Sutton, went off to Leith and set up as a shipbuilder only to fail in 1871, again owing money to M. & J. Allan. When Kirkpatrick & McIntyre of Port Glasgow closed in 1868 they were in arrears to the Allans to the tune of £53.19.10. They had just completed three barques, *River Avon 500/66*, *River Ganges 500/67* and *Lake Constance 500/67*. Another Port Glasgow shipyard, McFadyen & Co, closed in 1878 owing money to M. & J. Allan, their last sailing ships being *Battleaxe 775/74* and *Loch Cree 761/73*. McCulloch & Patterson, again of Port Glasgow, had them on the list of creditors when they failed in 1871. The last sailing ship which they built was the barque *Loch Urr 716/70* for D. & W. Sproat. A small shipyard further down the coast at Ardrossan was Barclay & Robertson and when they went out of business in 1877 M. & J. Allan were listed among the creditors for the sum of £4.5.0. It was not always small shipbuilders who went bankrupt. Dobie & Co. were one of the larger yards which could not make it. Their last launches were the barque *Loch Bredan 950/82* and the ship *Derry Castle 1367/83*, (4,13), and their figureheads were certainly carved by M. & J. Allan.

In 1893 M. & J. Allan were bought over by C. L. Dobbie. However, although entries were no longer made in the Trades Directories, Scotts of Greenock were still making payments in the name of M. & J. Allan up until 1900. At least one figurehead carved by this firm has survived, that of *Helen Denny 695/66* in the Museum of Transport in Glasgow and another 'possible', *Amphitrite 1708/82* aboard the *Cutty Sark*.

James Allan, junior, of Port Glasgow.   James Allan, junior, spent some years in Africa and when he returned to Port Glasgow in 1870 he set up in business as a ship carver in premises provided by his uncles in Glasgow, Messrs. M. & J. Allan, who also furnished him with the necessary tools. At one time he was making £150 per annum plus payments of about £50 from the Glasgow firm to meet expenses incurred on their behalf. In 1883 he was compelled to go into liquidation. He appears to have carved around 31 figureheads for the Robert Duncan yard (23) and oddly enough the last entry was for 1885, two years after his bankruptcy, presumably working for his uncles. Between 1873 and 1877 he cut carved work for Scotts of Greenock for at least 13 ships, including the Blue Funnel *Stentor 2025/75* and *Anchises 2025/75* for which he received £96.7.3. Other contracts were to provide decorative work for the Scott family's steam yachts, *Greta 46/77* for £8.10.0 and *Greta 57/78*, for £10.0.0. Both were named after a stream on the family estate and the latter had a demi-male figurehead.

19. *(Above)* James Nicol Fleming 993/69 *was built by Robert Duncan of Port Glasgow and had a figurehead of that gentleman cut by M. & J. Allan as part of a carving bill of £23.0.0. (Courtesy Alexander Turnbull Library, Wellington, New Zealand)*

19. *(Left) The figurehead of* Ann Gambles 465/62 *was typical of the "owner's wife" style of carving common on small merchantmen. She came from the workshop of Allan & Clotworthy. The ship herself was built by Williamson of Whitehaven. (Courtesy Whitehaven Museum.)*

Some of the old letter books have survived and these give some indication of the other carved work which a ship carver had to provide:

16 small capitals, carve and gild

5 large --do--

5 corner--do--

20 lengths of neck moulding, carve only

1 large capital, carve and gild

1 small --do--

Carve patterns for name boards for casting in iron, the back to be hollowed out.

For this order Allan ran into trouble with late delivery and the shipyard wrote complaining in strong terms. He also forgot to hollow out the name board patterns and had to go down to the shipyard to carry out the work. James Allan, jr. carved for some of the small yards on the Clyde. He produced carved work for McFadyen & Co. of Port Glasgow from at least 1875 until they went bankrupt in 1878, owing Allan £3.9.6. Allan himself was owed money by several shipyards when his business failed in 1883. Reid & Co. and Cunliffe & Dunlop, both of Port Glasgow, and Barclay Curle & Co of Glasgow , the last for only a small sum.

Allan & Laurie, Greenock. For several years the partnership of Allan & Laurie plied their trade in Greenock as ship carvers. Allan's first name is not known but his partner's full name was Robert Robertson Laurie. They started in 1855 and built up a business which paid out £400 to £500 per annum to nine employees. Around 1867 they transferred their business to Glasgow but in 1869 a fire destroyed their workshop. Laurie returned to Greenock where he went into business as a spirit dealer. He carried out one final piece of carving on a contract with Caird & Co. The spirit business failed in 1871 but the Trades Directories still carried his name as a carver as late as 1881. The Allan side of the partnership remains a mystery and his name is not mentioned after 1861. The cash books of Scotts of Greenock show entries for Allan & Laurie from 1858 to 1861 and R. R. Laurie from 1861 to 1864. The amounts paid out annually varied from £11.12.0 to £287.0.0.

Laurie must have been an accomplished carver as his reputation went beyond the banks of the Clyde. Laing of Sunderland sent him orders for three of their ships, *Aries 611/62*, for £128.3.6, *Lucerne 678/62*, £29.0.0, and *Coldstream 545/62*, £44.10.0. In 1858 Palmer's of Jarrow used some panelling from Laurie for one of their vessels. Family papers no longer in this country stated that "Laurie supplied work for many Clydeside yards as well as exporting figureheads to Canada around 1850 to 1870." Enquiries to the east coast museums of Canada brought no confirmation that such transactions took place but at least one report indicated that this did occur. A paragraph in the Illustrated London News in 29th. December 1860 stated that "*Great Australia 1661/60*, a clipper built by Stewart & Co. of St. John's, New Brunswick had a figurehead which had been carved in Britain and shipped out to Canada."

Allan & Clotworthy, Liverpool.(19).
Another member of the Allan 'Clan', Andrew Allan, left Greenock for Liverpool around 1846, working on his own until he went into partnership with Hugh Clotworthy in about 1857 to form Allan & Clotworthy.

That he was a skilled carver was confirmed years later when the son-in-law of the Liverpool carver William Dodd stated that: "Mr. Allan of Allan & Clotworthy was the finest carver I ever saw in my time." From their workshop came the figurehead of *James Baines 2515/54*. Mr.Baines was the owner of the American Black Ball Line of sailing ships and he came over to Liverpool where he sat for his likeness to be copied, dressed as an English gentleman with frock coat, stock collar, and bow tie. When the figurehead was completed it was put in a packing case and shipped to

20. *The newspapers usually paid little attention to the figurehead when reporting the launch of a vessel. Andrew Allan's must therefore have been outstanding to warrant this the following description of the figurehead which he cut for* Roscoe 172/48 *which was extracted from the Liverpool Courier and reprinted in the local Greenock newspaper as a tribute to one of her 'sons'.*

FIGURE CARVING.—We have had great pleasure in inspecting a full-length figure of William Roscoe, executed by Mr Andrew Allan, Wapping, and intended for a vessel now building in the Isle of Man, for James Aikin, Esq., of this town. Those who judge of figure-heads by the rude imitations of humanity which they see on most of the ships that frequent our docks, can form but a slight conception of the grace and beauty, the classical propriety, and artist-like character that belong to this choice production of Mr Allan's genius, which comes the nearest of anything we have seen to the strikingly characteristic portrait of "The Duke," by the same artist, which adorns the noble vessel of that name belonging to Mr George Kendall. The figure is about eight feet in height. The attitude is easy and natural, and at the same time dignified and commanding. The lofty brow, and large, well-proportioned head, fitly represent the seat of those vast intellectual energies with which the distinguished original was endowed. The eye, ardent and penetrating, and the mouth, which is relaxed into a benevolent smile, indicate the same correct observation and skilful handling, and together with the general contour of the features, constitute a likeness which it is impossible to mistake. The costume is in the Roman style, one arm supporting the folds of the toga, while the other depends gracefully by the side, the hand holding a scroll. In the management of the drapery Mr Allan has been peculiarly successful, displaying a taste and judgment that some of our most eminent sculptors have not always exhibited. Mr Allan, we believe, is a native of Greenock. He does honour to his birth-place, and will add to the reputation which the Clyde men already possess for excellence in the construction of vessels, the reputation of excellence in the ornamenting of them. — *Liverpool Courier.*

Boston to be fitted. The Harrison owned ship *Geologist 854/59* bore the full length figurehead of Hugh Miller the eminent geologist, carved by one of the partners. Royden's *Our Queen 461/60* carried a splendid gilt figure of Queen Victoria on her bows, carved in the same workshop. The partners executed carved work for other local shipyards, Clover, Vernon, Royden, Hart & Stinnett, Jordan and Jones & Quiggin (21). For the last named they carved some of their finest figureheads. From the hands of Allan & Clotworthy is reputed to have come a most unusual figurehead, that of *Devil 149/59*. Legend has it that two brothers were arguing over the choice of name for a new schooner. At last one of them lost his temper and shouted "call her the devil if you like" and *Devil* she became, with a fine full length figurehead of His Satanic Majesty with horns, hooves and a tail which came over his arm. Oddly enough, instead of being painted black it was painted gilt. The figurehead was fitted and was 'reconciled,' (i.e. adjusted in situ to suit the bow and bowsprit), by another carver called William Dodd who repaired it years later after a collision. After the schooner was broken up this remarkable figurehead was preserved for many years but finally disappeared. Ten years later, the same yard, Smith of Preston, built a schooner called *Sheitan* 140/69 whose figurehead represented the female devil Sheitan, who, in Chinese demonology, was the Goddess of Evil.

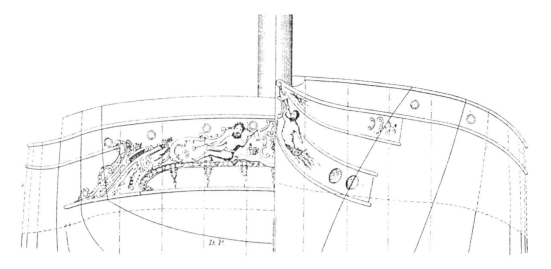

21. *Allan & Clotworthy have been specified as the carvers for Jones & Quiggin of Liverpool. In a book on Naval Architecture by W. J. M. Rankine there is a drawing of their* Formby 1271/63 *which shows the proposed carved work on the bow and stern of this sailing ship.*

Other orders came from the Cumberland coast shipyards including *Belted Will 812/63,* launched by J. Fell of Workington. The newspapers report stated that "the bows of *Belted Will* were adorned with a full length figure of the border chieftain whose deeds were recorded in song and story, executed in Liverpool in first rate style, his hand resting upon the hilt of his weapon, and clothed with armour befitting the period, by Messrs. Allan & Clotworthy, copied from a relic at Corby."

After 1873 the partnership seems to have split up, forming Allan & Sons, later Andrew Allan, and Hugh Clotworthy on his own as a ship carver and spirit dealer. In the 1877 Directory his place is taken by Alexander Clotworthy, ship carver, along with Andrew Clotworthy. The 1880 Gore's Directory contains an entry for "Thomas Allan, figurehead carver", possibly one of the sons of Andrew Allan.

William Allan, Greenock. William Allan is listed first in the Post Office Directory for 1837 as a carver, and in the 1842 voters' roll as a "carver and teacher of modelling." During 1842 he provided carved work valued at £9.9.0 for a barque being built in the short-lived yard of Thomson & Spiers of Greenock

William Allen, Jarrow. In the books of the Laing shipyard during 1861 to 1862 the name of William Allen of Jarrow appears against four vessels. Allen shared the work on *General Havelock 472/61* and *Lady Havelock 480/61* with George Tate, and Allen got the lion's share at £30.14.6 and

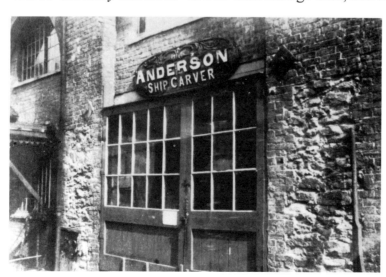

21. *Although when this photograph was taken the figurehead was a thing of the past, Thomas Anderson still proudly proclaimed himself on his shop sign to be a "Ship Carver" (Craig / Farr collection)*

22. *(Above) When* Greta 1190/74 *was built in Whitehaven, John Askew was the local carver. The figure is said to represent Robert Southey, the poet, while Greta is a stream in Cumberland whence Southey came.*

22. *(Right) The Caernaervon built brig* Hugh Roberts 181/76 *was wrecked in the Orkneys in 1890. The figurehead depicts the owner and he holds a scroll in his hand, a feature used by the carver when the subject was the owner or a political personality.*

£22.9.6 respectively. He had the other two contracts to himself with *Newburn 687/61* bringing him £19.2.0 and *Ville de Brest 638/62* a more profitable figure of £116.1.6.

John Robert Anderson. Bristol. (21). The Anderson family of Bristol came from Rotherhithe on the banks of the Thames where John Anderson (senior) was a " ship wood carver." He had intended to move to Bristol but died prematurely at the age of 34. (Family papers show that an Anderson carved at the Deptford Dockyard in 1779). His son John Robert Anderson, then 6 years old was sent to Bristol to live with his grandfather Robert Price Williams, himself a ship carver, and was in due course apprenticed to him. In 1862, at the age of 33 Anderson was made a partner in the firm which for a time took the title of Williams & Anderson and in 1868 John R. Anderson took over the business. In 1880 he moved to a workshop in Limekiln Dock Passage where in 1888, he started to carve ornamental work for fairgrounds including the horses for round-abouts for which he became famous. When his son Arthur Anderson took over the business it was mainly producing fairground carvings. In 1931 a newspaper recalled that the last figurehead carved by Anderson had been in 1914, a replacement for *Carib Prince 2047/93*, after providing one for *Kaffir Prince 2228/91*.

John Anderson, Newcastle. The 1821 Trades Directory shows a J. Anderson & Son, carvers and gilders in Newcastle. In 1830 Anderson carved the stern of *Elswick 265/30*, the first ship from the yard of H. S. Edwards of South Shields for the sum of £3.2.0. He carved a bust in American fir for No.15, *Viscount Melbourne 670/35* for £50.0.0, a price which must have included a considerable amount of carved work. It is probable that Anderson also carved for Nos. 2 to 14. His name was still entered in the 1865 Directory.

Thomas Anderson, South Shields. A guide to mid-19th. century South Shields refers to Thomas Anderson, a famous carver of ships' figureheads up the Black Bull Bank, Carpenter Street. His name appears in the Directories between 1845 and 1867, though in the later ones the address is given as Corporation Street. The 1828 Piggott Directory gives a Richard Anderson in Carpenter Street, presumably Thomas's father who may have been a ship carver. In the 1869 Directory a William Anderson is described as a carver but nothing has been found to indicate that he did ship carving.

John Askew, Whitehaven. In the Trades Directory for 1811 John Askew is entered as a "carver and gilder", while in the 1829 edition he is called a "ship carver." He died in 1845 but was succeeded by his son, also John, who died in 1881. Both men were well known on the North- East coast and although a considerable quantity of family papers have been preserved there is no information in them relating to the ship carving business (22).

Thos.& Jno. Brocklebank Ltd. were a well-known shipping company. Less well known is the fact that they were also shipbuilders occupying a yard in Whitehaven from 1788 until 1865. The surviving company records which span a period 1807 to 1865 show that from at least 1807 up to 1858 John Askew, both father and son, were the sole ship carvers to the Brocklebank yard and during this period 108 vessels were launched, mainly of a size which would have had figureheads. In the records only a few ships are named but there is sufficient to give an idea of the Askew's charges. *Caroline 237/10*, a ship, £21.0.0. *Aimwell 250/13*, a brig, £6.10.0. *Balfour 310/09*, a brig, £2.19.0. Several times the entry in the journal simply states "sundries", but for these a great deal of money changed hands. 1816- £61.0.0, 1818- "51.6.0, 1825- £60.10.0. The last entry under their name was the only one to give any detail:

31st. May 1858. No. 143. Carving two headboards, name boards, gilding	£4.10.0.
Oak quarters and tail pieces	2. 0.0.
12 comp. caps for cabins	12.0.
Carved work on stern	15.15.0.

The only vessel launched by Brocklebank's with a family name was *Thomas Brocklebank 629/47*, a ship. A famous name which was commemorated was that of the founder of the Penny Post for the schooner *Roland Hill 65/44*. Usually the carver would cut a good likeness of his subject but in one case at least the newspaper reporter thought otherwise, for, on the 30th. December 1834 when he attended the launch of *Earl of Lonsdale 230/34*, he wrote: "She has a very elegant figurehead, representing the Earl of Lonsdale in his robes and collar of the Star and Garter, which has only one fault, (though some persons may think it no fault) that it does not bear the remotest resemblance to

23. *Scott's of Greenock built* Oamaru 1306/74 *for the New Zealand trade and James Allan, junior, carved the figurehead as part of a contract worth £78.7.10.*
(Courtesy Alexander Turnbull Library, Wellington, New Zealand)

23. *John Gambles was a ship owner and for his* John Gambles 1066/74 *he had a likeness of himself carved for her bow. James Brooker has been credited with cutting this figure but since he was long dead it is likely that it was George Brooker's work. (Whitehaven Museum)*

his Lordship's figure or face." One assumes from this that John Askew had been kind to His Lordship and had flattered him in these respects.

The Askews must have had many other customers as it is clear that they had a prosperous business judging from the number of stocks and shares which had to be disposed of when the estate was cleared up after the latter's death. When John Askew died the contents of his workshop were sold at auction and the list of items filled a notebook. The list included a number of carved wood objects which were disposed of at ridiculously low prices:

Carved fish	7d.
Coat of Arms	3/-
Figurehead	3/-
Figurehead	3/-
Two pieces of carving	6d.
Bunch of Grapes	7d.

There were dozens of plaster figures in the schedule of contents and it is possible that, like James Law of Dundee, John Askew made use of these as models for his figureheads. When the Brocklebank shipyard dispensed with their services in about 1858 their place was taken by Jonathan Shepherd.

Benjamin Smith Bailes, Sunderland.   Bailes' name appears only twice in the shipbuilding records which have survived. He received £14.5.0 from the Laing Yard for the carved work for their steamer *Contest 524/79* and in 1870 Bartrams paid him £11.5.0 for "carved work" for a vessel, the name of which was not given.

Batton & Glover, London. (Battin or Betton).   *Earl of Grenville 180/1755* was owned by Baisley of London and in 1768 she had repairs carried out by a carver named Battin for 11/6. In 1770 Betton, carver, worked on her for 18/-. In 1794 Batton & Glover cut carved work for the East India Company ship *Arniston 1433/94*, built by Barnard & Co. of Deptford, including the coat of arms of the Lord Advocate of Scotland on her stern. They also renovated her decorative work in 1799 after her nineteen month round voyage to China,

Bond of Bideford.   Bond is described in local books as a "well known figurehead carver in Devon." *Rose of Torridge 149/75*, the heroine of Kingsley's book, Westward Ho!., is preserved aboard the *Cutty Sark* and she was 'cut' by either Bond or another well known local carver, Petherwick. When the steam yacht *Violette 57/77* was built by Cox of Bideford she was fitted with a figurehead carved by Bond.

Richard S. Branfoot, Sunderland.   In 1850 in the local directory there was a carving concern called Branfoot & Swan, but there was also an R.S.Branfoot. As this was the last time that Swan's name appeared it is possible that the partnership split up during that year. In the 1851 census Branfoot was described as " an apprentice carver and gilder aged 24, unmarried." Rather old for an apprentice in those days. Between 1864 and 1865 Branfoot carried out a number of small jobs for the Bartram yard, but only for three of those contracts was the vessel named. *George Bartram 284/65*, carved work, £7.0.0, *Northumbria 295/65*, figurehead and carved work, £5.12.6, and *Sarah Jane 365/68*, carved work, £11.18.0. One of the orders for an unspecified ship was a bit more detailed, viz. 1866, carved work, painted and gilded, scroll head and shield, £7.0.0., painting and gilding a ship model 12/6.

W. H. Bridges, Sunderland.   William Henry Bridges was described in the directories as a "carver and gilder" in 1850 and as a "ship and sign carver" in 1869. He performed two tasks for Laing's, carving the stern galleries for *Pyrenees 832/51* for £18.10.0 and *Vimiera 1037/51* for

£27.10.0. The latter was described in the London Illustrated News as "consisting of tastefully arranged groups of banners etc., in the centre of which is a shield with a lion rampant, the whole executed in first-rate style."

British Charrier Carving Co.   The location of this company is not known but it is on record that they were paid £28.15.5. by Scotts of Greenock for their share of the work of the decorative carvings on the steam yacht *Margarita 1792/00*. In the cost books of Russell of Port Glasgow there is an entry against ship No.523, *Laura 6125/07* where the cost of the carved work was shared between John Roberts and "The Charrier & Marbut Carving Co."

George Brooker, Workington.   Little is known of George Brooker, son of a carpenter, save that he was born in Liverpool in 1824 and that by the time he was 57 years old he had retired. He was described as a "ship and ornamental carver and gilder", and must have had a good business at some time as he was involved in part ownership of ships. However, one comment has come down to us out of the past: "George Brooker carved figureheads for windjammers. He was said to have been so clever that he could have knocked out an Aphrodite with a hatchet." There is in the museum at Whitehaven an old slide showing the figurehead of *John Gambles 1027/74*, built in Harrington, which credits James Brooker with the carving. As James Brooker had died about fourteen years earlier it is fair to assume that in fact it was George Brooker who had cut the figurehead (23).

James Brooker, Maryport.   James Brooker was a well known ship carver on the Cumberland coast and the local newspapers sometimes included in their launch reports details of the figureheads which Brooker cut. He came from Liverpool where he served an apprenticeship from 1828 under Archibald Robertson and in 1842, describing himself as a sculptor and carver, he took a grant of land in Maryport and built a workshop in Church Street. On the lintel above the door he carved a replica of the Lion of Lucerne, designed by Thorwaldsen and carved in the rocks by Lake Lucerne by a Swiss sculptor in 1821. It seems likely that he began his career earlier than this, for, when the barque *Blair 333/38* was launched from Ritson's yard the newspaper reported that the figurehead and taffrail had been carved by J. Brookman, certainly a misprint for Brooker. He carved figureheads for Lumley, Kennedy including *Warlock 330/40*, ornamented with a "full length figurehead and elaborately carved stern", and *Enchantress 284/41* and *Syren 314/40*, both with "well executed full length female figures." Other customers were Keswick Wood of Maryport, Ritson's (26) and the Whitehaven Shipbuilding Company. One of his early works was the full length figure of Gilbert Henderson, Recorder of Liverpool for the ship *Recorder 330/40*, built in Maryport by Keswick Wood, with stern decorations including the figure of Justice. In 1851 Charles Lamport of Workington launched *Dinapore 780/51* and the papers waxed lyrical about the carvings: "She is the largest ship that has been launched in Cumberland and is classed A.1. at Lloyds for nine years. Her bow is adorned with two full length and lifelike figures by James Brooker. The idea originated by seeing a print of Venus and Adonis. The youth is represented in hunter's garb, clasping a dart in his right hand extended, while the female endeavours as it were to restrain him from incurring the varied dangers of his intended enterprise. Though Mr. Brooker executed this fine carving at very short notice, he succeeded in imparting to the figures in their attitude and drapery a degree of graceful carelessness of which it is difficult to furnish an adequate description." In the same year James Brooker received a testimonial from Wood's yard and a medal awarded at the Crystal Palace Exhibition of 1851. The fame of James Brooker spread and he was called on by Laing of Sunderland to carve figureheads for at least 18 of their ships including Duncan Dunbar's *Talavera 916/50*, figurehead and carved work, £11.10.8, *Pyrenees 832/51*, with a figure of the Duke of Wellington, £10.13.4, *Vimiera 1037/51*, had Fame blowing a trumpet, and *Dunbar 1167/54*, carried a lion, £17.5.0. (Several of Dunbar's ships had lion figureheads). On the last named the carving of the stern decorations were done by William Bridges of Sunderland. The Brocklebank shipyard in Whitehaven employed John Askew as their sole carver for nigh on fifty years but James Brooker is reported to

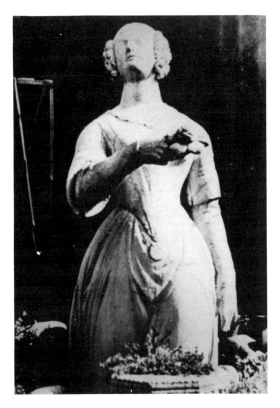

26. Mary Ann Johnston 357/48 *was built by Ritson of Maryport for Captain Fawcett and he had James Brooker carve a likeness of his sister to adorn her bows. This figurehead survived locally until 1966.*

26. *This sketch shows one of the few signed figureheads which are known and it bears the inscription "J. Brooker, M'pt." Two possibles are ships built by James Laing of Sunderland, Anglia 570/49 and* Mercia 567/50. *(Sketch by R. Hunter.*

have carved the figurehead for their *Martaban 852/52*, "a full length female figure in asiatic costume." On the 14th. of December 1853 Brooker closed his workshop and all the furniture and fittings were sold. He moved north to Glasgow where he announced his arrival with an advertisement in the Post Office Directory (26).

It is probable that Glasgow had enough local carvers without a stranger starting up for Brooker was on the move again within a year, this time to Sunderland where his reception was much better. In the records in Glasgow only one account has been traced where J. & G. Thompson of Clydebank paid out on two small bills totalling £31.10.0. In Sunderland he carved for at least eight

of the ships built by Laing, again including vessels for Duncan Dunbar. *La Hogue 1300/55*, £20.10.0. and *Asia 1093/58*, £35.16.0. This was the last entry made against Brooker's name. Despite his desertion of the Cumberland coast Brooker continued to receive orders from his old customers there. In 1858 Brooker placed an advertisement in the local directory which read almost word for word the same as the Glasgow one but printed with much more flourish. It is surprising that he did not obtain testimonials from his Sunderland customers. In the museum at Gothenburg there is an unknown figurehead signed "J.Brooker, M'pt." which has removable arms and weapons, a feature commonly found on top

JAMES BROOKER

BEGS to announce to the Shipbuilders of the Clyde and its Vicinity, that he has commenced

SHIP AND ORNAMENTAL CARVING,

IN EVERY VARIETY,

AT

109 HYDEPARK STREET,

and, having been in business in Cumberland for twenty years, hopes, by quality of Work and punctuality, to merit a share of Public patronage.

The following are a few of the numerous Testimonials J. B. has received:—

"Maryport, 21st July, 1846.

" We have much pleasure in certifying that we have for many years employed Mr. Jas. Brooker in Carving Figure Heads and Sterns, and all other Carved Work belonging to Vessels and that we consider him inferior to none, but superior to most in that Art. We feel confident that he will give satisfaction to those who may employ him.

"K. WOOD & SONS, Shipbuilders."

———

(*From the " Whitehaven Herald," May 16, 1846.*)

Respecting the launching of a new Vessel named the 'Lord Hardinge,' the Editor thus writes :—" She has a finely-executed and elaborately-defined full-length portrait of that gallant soldier and wise statesman, in the full uniform of a field-marshal, and having all his newly-acquired badges of honour conspicuously set forth, as a figure-head. Also a beautiful medallion of the gallant General cut in the stern carvings, with other appropriate devices. We understand that the representation of the great warrior is a very striking one. It is, in our opinion, as fine a piece of workmanship as ever we saw from the chisel of that eminent carver, Mr. Brooker of Maryport."

class figureheads where projecting parts could be lost or damaged at sea. Very few figureheads were signed by their carver and the fact that this one bears Brooker's name suggests that it was carved at Maryport before 1853, for a yard elsewhere, possibly Sunderland (26). One of his last creations must have been *Mary Lee 465/59*, built by Ritson in Maryport. Early in 1860, now penniless and with his health and mind affected, Brooker was admitted to the workhouse and then to an asylum where he died on 13th. March 1860 as a result of injuries inflicted by the keeper.

William Brooker, Sunderland. When James Brooker died he left behind him a son, William, who followed his father in the ship carver's trade. The ledgers of the Laing yard contain entries against his name for five vessels for small amounts, ranging from *Biddick 640/64* for £5.0.0 to *Onega 856/64* for £16.0.0. He also provided carved work for two Doxford vessels, *Diamond 399/63* and *Cochrane 399/63* at a cost of £5 5.0.

Bryson & Co, Sunderland. In 1873 Bryson & Co. shared a couple of contracts with Joseph Melvin for two steamers for the Laing yard, *Khiva 2609/73* and *Kasagar 2621/73*. The decorative work must have been quite lavish as they received £79.12.0 and £81.9.0 for their part.

John Buchan, Greenock. The Buchan family of Greenock were all in the carving and gilding business. In the 1881 census there are entries for John Buchan, aged 46, gilder, John Buchan, aged 22, carver, and Walter Buchan, aged 19, gilder. During 1879 to 1881 Russells shipyard of Port Glasgow paid them to provide carved work for nine of their ships, including *Peebleshire 866/79*, figurehead at £4.5.0, trailboards for £1.5.0, and general carving £8.9.10, all ascribed to John Buchan. In 1881 they were relegated to doing only general carved work. In the Trades Directories John Buchan was making entries until 1900 under " wood carver."

Thomas Burrough, Deptford. Thomas Burrough was the Master Carver for the naval yards at Deptford and Woolwich. His workshop also took in work for merchant ships as an old note book shows. The writer had made entries about ships being built at various yards on the banks of the Thames and there were two references where the carver's name is mentioned. "1752. Cost of building a sloop for the African trade......to Thomas Burrough, carver £10.0.0." "1755. To price of building a ship for Captain Hill for the Lisbon trade.....to Thomas Burrough, carver £20.0.0." The shipyards were not named.

William Calder, Greenock. One of the earliest carvers in Greenock was William Calder, entered in the 1832 directory as a "ship carver". The 1841 census shows him as a "ship carver", aged 40, and also his son Henry Calder, aged 20, also a "ship carver". Thomson & Spiers who operated a shipyard in Greenock from 1840 to 1842 gave them an order for a carved stern board for the barque *Janet Wilson 280/42* worth £4.10.0 and carved work for a brig valued at £5.15.0. Calder also cut the carved work for their brig *Robertina 213/43*. Another small yard, Murress & Clarke of Greenock, employed William Calder to provide carved work for their last orders, the ship *Brooksby 505/43* and a brig *Adam Smith 223/44*.

Archibald Campbell, Greenock. Born in 1789, Archibald Campbell was one of the original ship carvers in the Clyde area. In 1814 when the Greenock shipbuilder David Porter went into liquidation his records show that he owed Campbell £18.10.8. In 1826 he was submitting invoices to Denny of Dumbarton for "carved timber", £8.0.0, in 1828 for "wood and carving work", £7.16.0 and in 1834 for "carving trailboards for a brig, £3.19.0." He died in 1841 but his son Archibald continued to put entries in the Trades Directory as a "gilder" until 1846. It must have been his son who cut the carved work in 1842 for the last vessel built at the yard of Robert Duncan of Greenock who died in 1841, a schooner, which fetched Campbell £11.7.0. (It was Robert Duncan's son who founded his own better known shipyard in 1862.)

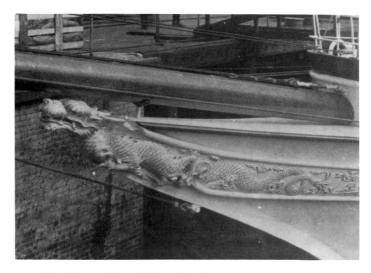

28. *(Above). Not all figureheads were serious. When John Crawford carved this figurehead for the steam yacht* Sapphire *1208/12, built by John Brown of Clydebank, he was creating something which must have been the subject of much comment. (Courtesy Glasgow University, Business Records Department).*

28. *(Left). When Dennison's of Sunderland launched the barque* Lowestoft *303/66 they placed on her bow a most unusual figurehead, the caricature of a fish as being appropriate to her name. She was lost off the mouth of the Tyne and her figurehead is preserved in the Tynemouth Life Brigade House.*

Alexander Chalmers, Edinburgh.   In 1876 John Scott & Son of Inverkeithing started bankruptcy proceedings and Alexander Chalmers was called on to complete the carved work on a three-masted schooner for £16.10.0, and to provide carved work for their Yard No. 55 at a cost of £14.2.7. There had been a Chalmers in Edinburgh in the carving and gilding business since 1821.

Peter Christie, Greenock.   There was working in Greenock a Peter Christie who was described in the 1841 census as a "carver", aged 54, but it is his son Peter whom we know to have been a ship carver. In 1851, aged 45, he was recorded as being "a master carver employing one man, (his son Peter), and an apprentice carver." In 1861 the young Peter apparently left his father and was living away from home now working as wood carver. The earliest contract found was £6.10.0 for a figurehead for the barque *Duke of Portland 533/42* from the short lived yard of Thomson & Spiers of Greenock. In 1843 James McMillan, shipbuilder, Greenock went into receivership and it was Peter Christie who was called on to execute the carved work on the two vessels which were on the stocks, the barque *Aberfoyle 416/43,* £3.10.0. carved work on the stem, and a brig, possibly called *Agnes,* £9.0.0, figurehead and trailboards. Another yard in Port Glasgow which survived only a few years was that of Charles Wood who, when they went out of business in 1845, owed Christie £40.18.8. Three ships are mentioned in the documents, *Caledonia 1150/40, Tay 1858/41* and *Marion.* The records of Scotts of Greenock show that Peter Christie carried out considerable contracts between 1851 and 1866, but in only one case is the ship's name given in the ledgers, that of *Campo Idoglio 601/62* for the sum of £188.0.0. When *Atrato 3466/53* was launched at the yard of Caird & Co. of Greenock the newspapers reported that "her bow was surmounted by a spirited representation of an Indian deity, the work of Mr. Peter Christie of Greenock." There are no other shipyard records and no entries in the directories after 1881. However, as late as 1920 the name of Neil Christie appears in the Russell & Co. ledgers against an entry for "other carved work". One of Peter Christie's employees was a man named Martin Harley, (about 1849-1852). Above Port Glasgow between the wars there was a park called Auchmountain Glen in which a number of figureheads were set for decoration and it has been claimed that Harley carved some of these.

David Cockburn, South Shields. No record of David Cockburn has been found other than this single advertisement in the Ward's Directory in 1855. (29).

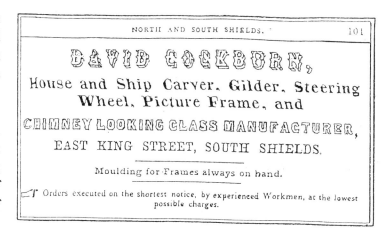

NORTH AND SOUTH SHIELDS. 101

DAVID COCKBURN,

House and Ship Carver, Gilder, Steering Wheel, Picture Frame, and

CHIMNEY LOOKING GLASS MANUFACTURER,

EAST KING STREET, SOUTH SHIELDS.

Moulding for Frames always on hand.

☞ Orders executed on the shortest notice, by experienced Workmen, at the lowest possible charges.

Charles Cook, Aberdeen. There is only one entry in the cost books of Hall of Aberdeen against Charles Cook for a small amount of carving for *Dart 88/44* with a value of 10/-.

Dick Cowell, Southampton. In Southampton the Oswald, Mordaunt & Co. shipyard appears to have employed their own carver for some time, a craftsman by the name of Dick Cowell. In the book " Champion of Sail " he is recorded as having carved the figureheads for many of their ships. Oswald, Mordaunt built Leyland's *Scottish Dales 2059/83, Scottish Hills 2059/83* and *Scottish Lochs 2466/88* and Cowell carved for one of them a figurehead representing R. W. Leyland's daughter. It must have been well executed as it was highly praised and the carver received a gratuity from the young lady's proud father.

John Crawford, Glasgow. John Crawford's name was entered for the first time in the directories in 1875 when he was 26 years old. In the 1881 census he is described as "a master carver employing 2 men and 2 boys." His name appears in several shipyard records but only for J. & G. Thomson of Clydebank does he seem to have carried out regular work (28). From 1890 to 1893 the contracts were lucrative with annual payments ranging from £190 to £419. From 1899 to 1902 Crawford was once more receiving orders which again brought in good money from £217 to £457 each year. Only two ship's names are mentioned, *City of New York 10499/90*, (30), and as late as 1918, *H.M.S.Hood,* for which he provided internal carved work to a value of £68.0.0. For Russell & Co. of Port Glasgow he cut one figurehead, that of *Henry Swayne 725/82* for which they paid him £4.5.0. Denny of Dumbarton made a payment to him in 1881 for £5.15.0. for unspecified work. He was still carving after 1900 and provided figureheads for two steam yachts from the Fairfield yard at Govan. *Queen of Scots 605/04* for £22.10.0 and *Narcissus 816/05* for £21.10.0. Scotts of Greenock went to him for internal carved work for their steam yacht *Margarita 1792/00* when he received £30.15.0 out of a total bill for carved work of £103.9.11. He cut the external carved work for another Scotts' steam yacht, *Cassandra 1227/08* for £20.15.0. The wood for this job cost £7.16.9 and "sawing the figurehead" cost £3.13.3. The ship owners William Thomson of Dundee continued to fit figureheads long after they introduced steamships to their fleet. *Benmohr 4806/12* was one of the last, launched from Scott's yard, with carved work by Crawford. *Benmohr* was sunk in October 1914 by the raider *Emden.*

There was a Crawford & Co. in the directories as late as 1930, as carvers and gilders, and in fact that year they carved a figurehead for the steam yacht *Rover 1851/30* launched from Alexander Stephen's yard in Govan, charging £44.0.0. for the figurehead and £159.0.0. for the internal work. In the directory John Crawford described himself as "a craftsman".

Robert Williams Culmore, London. Son of a block maker, Robert Culmore appears in the Directories from 1856 until 1875 as a "ship carver." The 1851 census gave his age as 33.

Charles Dark, London. No records have survived to show what work Dark did in the London area, but his figureheads were of sufficiently high quality to attract the attention of Hall's of Aberdeen. During a period between 1840 and 1848 he provided carved work for no less than 39

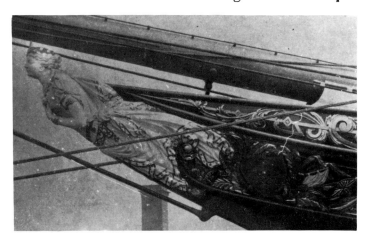

30. *(Above). The figurehead which John Crawford carved for J. & G. Thomson's* City of New York 10499/90 *was a thing of beauty as was the complex carving of the trailboards. (Courtesy Glasgow University Business Records Department)*

30. *(Right). Quite plain by comparison is the figurehead of* Sunset 37 t.m/87. *She is only 18" long and came from a schooner yacht built as* Zaimph *in east Donyland, near Colchester. One fault she has is that her arms are too heavy for the body.*

vessels, with 33 contracts for figureheads and 6 for carved work. The vessels ranged from a small schooner, *Matchless 170/46* with a female figure costing £1.15.0, to full rigged ships like *Glentanner 610/42* which brought him £30.11.0. Although he was a London carver working for an Aberdeen yard only four of the ships were destined for London owners. The others were built for ports which had their own established ship carvers including *Humayoon 530/42* for Greenock, £25.2.0 and *William Panton 170/45* for Liverpool, £23.0.0.

G. L. Davidson, Newcastle.   In 1868 G. L. Davidson executed the figurehead and the carved work for *Waterlily 379/68*, built in the Bartram yard, for which he was paid £10.0.0.

Charles Lizars Dobbie, Glasgow.   Around 1862 Charles Lizars Dobbie (aged about 24) took over the old established firm of William Shanks, formerly Kay & Shanks. He expanded the business and by 1881 was employing 18 men and 8 boys in a variety of carved work. Although his predecessor had been favoured with many orders from Denny of Dumbarton, Dobbie only provided carved work for four of their vessels, *Irene 887/63* for which he was paid £85.0.0, *Kentucky 1153/64*, £126.16.0, *Corea 874/64*, £156.9.0 and *Oriental 1480/66*, £69.10.0. He must have been sorry to lose such expensive contracts. However, this loss was compensated by the orders which he was given by Elder of Govan, later Fairfield (32). Available records show that between 1866 and 1894 he provided figureheads and carved work for at least 58 vessels covering everything from sailing yachts to battleships. The cutter yacht *Daphne 61/79* cost £10.10.2, while the steam yacht *Lady Torfrida 363/90* brought in £53.12.8. The composite ship *Carrick Castle 904/68* cannot have had much of a figurehead as Dobbie only charged £2.14.2, but he took £24.0.10 for the internal carving. The paddle steamer *Panama 1642/66* had a figurehead costing £3.12.0. while the rest of the decorative carving was priced at £132.11.11. The highest cost was for *S.S.Werra 5012/82* which was worth £293.6.5. Not to be forgotten was the circular yacht *Livadia 7262/80* which was extensively decorated at a cost of £275.18.0. In those days even warships carried a considerable amount of carved work and in 1878 Elder's paid out £61.0.0 for *H.M.S. Nelson 7473/76*, an armoured frigate, and £8.12.6. for *H.M.S. Curacao 2380/78*, a corvette. In 1893 Dobbie took over the business of M. & J. Allan. C. L. Dobbie died in 1910 and in his obituary was described as a" Ship carver, gilder and wood letter maker." His was one of the few ship carving businesses to receive any kind of publicity when a paragraph appeared in a volume called "Glasgow and its Environments " which covered the activities of various businesses. The article described their work on model figureheads for ship models for an exhibition. An early issue reported that "They also carved a great number of figureheads for vessels. At one time the carving of figureheads was a matter of vital importance, and Jack Tar had a violent objection to sailing with any vessel whose figurehead he happened to disapprove of. This feeling has to a great extent died out, in this country at least, but still artistic tastes prompt ship builders to a due observance of elegance in the appearance of their vessels. These figures are carved from wood but are painted to resemble stone." A later version of the paragraph in " Glasgow and its Environs " is reproduced below. J. & G. Thomson came to him between 1890 and 1893 but the cost ledgers do not name any ships. Scotts of Greenock placed orders for the *Souerah 751/68* worth £10.4.0. The records which have survived for Stephen's of Linthouse only span 1881 to 1903, but from 1881 to 1895 C. L. Dobbie was the sole carving company employed by them. Most of the vessels were steamers but Dobbie did cut figureheads for the steel ships *Carradale 1982/89* and *Fascadale 2083/90* for £5.10.0 each. One of the steamers, *Benlarig 2265/81*, also had a figurehead. For McKie & Thomson they carved an unusual figurehead for *Dayspring 160/95*, (34), a mission ship for the South Pacific, portraying a young lady with her right arm outstretched, holding a bible. Work was undertaken for yards outwith Glasgow including two which went into receivership owing Dobbie money. D. & A. Fullerton of Ayr closed in 1870 with a debt of £1.10.11 and Black & Noble of Montrose failed in 1877 with £5.3.6 outstanding. In 1893 C. L. Dobbie took over the business of M. & J. Allan. C. L. Dobbie died in 1910 and in his obituary was described as a " Ship carver. gilder and wood letter maker."

C. L. DOBBIE & SON, Ship, Ornamental, and Architectural Carvers and Gilders, 386, Paisley Road, S.S., Glasgow.

FOREMOST amongst the industrial arts which have contributed to the commercial progress of this great northern centre, and which have been prominently associated with its material prosperity, must be mentioned the various branches of ship, ornamental, and architectural carving and gilding as represented by the eminent firm of Messrs. C. L. Dobbie and Son, whose widely-known establishment, 386, Paisley Road, S.S., Glasgow, supplies the subject of this review. The business is of very old standing, having been founded in Fox Street upwards of 60 years ago by Mr. Thomas Kay, who subsequently removed to Maxwell Street, and was, some years afterwards, succeeded by his foreman, the late Mr. William Shanks, the latter gentleman's interest reverting, many years ago, to the present proprietors. The premises occupied by Messrs. Dobbie are of extensive proportions, and comprise spacious ground floor workshops, conveniently arranged, presenting every facility for the economical and effective working of the various departments of the business. The services of a large staff of skilled designers and workmen are here engaged in the operative processes of carving and gilding every description of ship, ornamental, and architectural work, of which the leading *specialté* is the execution of carved Figure Heads and other designs for the ornamentation of ships, yachts, and other sea-going craft. It is worthy of note, in connection with this department of the firm's operations, that these gentlemen were honoured with the order for the execution of much of the carving and gilded work used in the construction of that triumph of the ship-builders' art, the luxurious steam yacht the " Livadia," which was built, at an almost fabulous cost, at the order of the late Czar of Russia, by Messrs. John Elder and Co., and which for the artistic splendour of its internal fittings has had no parallel in the history of marine architecture.

Equal activity is observable in the other departments of the business, such as in Figure Heads, of which many fine examples are turned out; and especially in model carving for ship models, now such a feature in our various Exhibitions; also in patterns for casting. The business of Messrs. Dobbie and Son is managed under their personal supervision, and includes the most notable shipbuilders, architects, and iron-founders in and around the district, and their high reputation has been gained by the exercise of the greatest artistic skill in the execution of all orders entrusted to them for completion, and by the energy and ability they have consistently manifested in the successful development of this important and prosperous industrial undertaking.

William Dodd, Liverpool. William Dodd was a well known ship carver in the late 19th. century. He served his apprenticeship with A. & R. Robertson and afterwards worked for Allan & Clotworthy. He cut the figurehead for the sailing ship *Slieve Donard 1498/59* built by T. Vernon of Liverpool. He is reputed to have carved the figureheads for the Inman liners *City of Limerick 1529/55, City of Brussels 3081/69* and *City of Antwerp 2391/67*, all of which were built in Glasgow for their Liverpool owners. William Dodd also helped with the carved work for many Isle of Man steamers such as *Manx Fairy 400/53*. The ill-fated *Royal Charter 2719/65* was another vessel on whose carved work he was employed. She had a full male figure with a helmet on his head, with wings extending from each side and wings on his heels. It was Mr. Dodd who was sent to Preston to 'reconcile' the figurehead of the schooner *Devil 149/68*, that is to fit it on the bow and ensure that the attitude was correct and that it did not interfere with the rigging. When the figurehead was damaged some years later Mr. Dodd was sent down to the dock to carry out the necessary repairs, being subjected to a barrage of ribald comments while he worked. William Dodd must have been one of the last of the old figurehead carvers as he was still alive in 1921. In the Shire booklet on figureheads there appears a sketch entitled *Denmark*, drawn by Wm. Dodd, showing a proposed figurehead probably for a vessel 3724/66 built in Stockton for Liverpool owners. In the 1920s a series of articles in a Liverpool newspaper contained a photograph of a self portrait bust of William Dodd carved using his reflection in a mirror (32).

32. Sketch of bust of William Dodd by Richard Hunter taken from an old photograph in a Liverpool newspaper.

William Doig, Newcastle.   William Doig, a Scot, worked in Newcastle as a ship carver and gilder from about 1851 to 1867. In 1858 the firm's title was given as "Doig & Taylor, ship carvers". Possibly this was the James Taylor who later set up on his own. Doig was joined in the business by his son John.

William Drysdale, Glasgow.   In 1889 at the age of 54, William Drysdale moved from Dumbarton to Glasgow and put an entry in the Post Office Directory giving his business as "ship, cabinet, and architectural carver". However, this was the only time that he claimed to be a ship carver as in the following years he described himself simply as a "wood carver".

Andrew Duncan, Garmouth.   From 1840 until 1910 the firm of Andrew Duncan manufactured blocks and ironwork for locally built ships. In 1867 a local newspaper recorded that they were now in the business of ship carving with part of the workshop given over to the cutting of figureheads, scrolls and other devices (64).

Shon Edwards, Portmadoc.   Shon Edwards carved extensively for sailing ships built at Portmadoc and from his skilful chisel came figureheads, catheads, and sternboards(64). One of his most outstanding creations was the figurehead which he cut for *Pride of Wales 298/69*. The figure represented the owner's daughter Jenny Morris in a silk dress and buckled shoes, holding a rose in her outstretched right hand. The figure stood with one foot slightly advanced, on a plinth on the stem of the vessel. The outstretched arm was demountable and could be removed when proceeding to sea on a long voyage and placed in a specially made mahogany box. The stern was a magnificent

32. *The sketch for the figurehead and trail boards for the barque* Pass of Melfort 2196/91 *which was built in the Fairfield yard in Glasgow was drawn by the shipyard in pencil. The trail boards contain much detail, of significance at the time, but not to us. It was C. L. Dobbie who carved the figurehead. (Courtesy Strathclyde Regional Archives)*

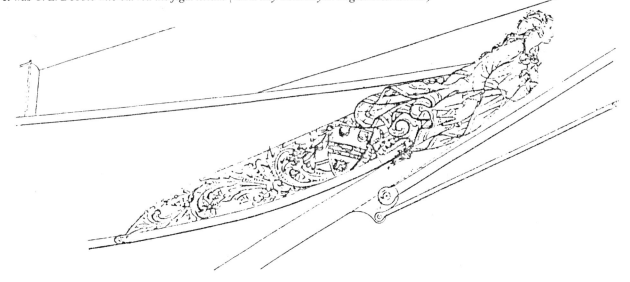

piece of carving. The *Pride of Wales* was to start her career in the Indian Ocean and so the stern portrayed animals in a jungle of reeds and grasses. Another product of the Edwards chisel was a bust on *Cadwalader Jones 103/78*, dressed in a tunic, with a sash bearing decorative badges, while the hands were encased in white gloves.

Alexander Pettigrew Elder, London, Sunderland and Glasgow. Elder was born in Dundee in 1828 and first appears in London in 1853 when he set up business as a ship carver in Limehouse. No record has been found of any work which he may have done for yards in London but he attracted the attention of James Laing of Sunderland who ordered from him figureheads for *Amity 607/54*, which cost £17.2.6, *Great Northern 578/54*, £13.17.6, and *Alfred 585/54*, £13.15.0. In 1863

he left London and moved up to Sunderland where he continued to work for the Laing yard, completing for them decorative carving for some 13 vessels during the period 1863 to 1868. They paid quite well and the costs varied from £3.4.0 for *Narva 1282/66* to £40.5.0 for *Hiogo 738/65*.

Around 1869 Elder was on the move again, this time to the Clyde where he had addresses in Port Glasgow and in Glasgow. He disappears from the directories in 1886. Elder is one of the few carvers for whom personal records have been preserved. The National Maritime Museum holds his sketch book with 53 drawings of figureheads and 12 stern boards. There is one sketch in the book which bears the stamp of Oswald, one of the little known shipbuilders in London, and the date 1866 and he may have done work for them at some time. A few sketches bear a vessel's name and some 'possibles' are *Cingalese 698/69* London & Glasgow S. B. Co., *Abergeldie 1152/69* Duthie, Aberdeen. Elder attempted with little success to get himself on to the list of carvers for the Royal Navy.

Details are given under ' Naval Carvers.'

33. A. P. Elder himself, looking very prosperous.

George Faldo, London. For a short time Faldo was on the list of carvers approved by the Admiralty and details are given under 'Naval Carvers.' In a letter which he wrote in 1832 he claimed that he had been in the ship carving business for 24 years himself, and his family before that. Although his name appears in the directories from 1808 to 1861 little has been found of any work carried out by the Faldo family for Thames-side shipyards. In 1837 the East India Company purchased *Waterford 418/36* which had recently gone aground. Renamed *Semiramis* she was put in the hands of Wigram & Green for repair and George Faldo was appointed to carve the Company arms on the taffrail with palms and other decorations on either side. An account for £4.0.0 was submitted by George Faldo to a ship owner in the West Country in 1855 for the supply of a three quarter figurehead of a lady, including timber, for a brig called *Dynamene 170/18* built in 1818 and lengthened in 1855. In the West Country it was common practice for the owner to supply the figurehead which the shipyard then fitted. His son Robert is entered from 1851 at a different address, but he moved into his father's premises in about 1861 carrying on the ship carving business. Faldo worked in partnership with another carver named Overton between 1817 and 1829. It is understood that Faldo's family name had originally been Faldonetti.

Richard Farrington, Newcastle. Farrington's name appears in the directories as early as 1778 as a carver and gilder. In the Bowes Museum, Barnard Castle there is a cellarette and on its

34. *(Above). C. L. Dobbie carved this expressive figurehead for the Mission steamer* Dayspring 160/95, *a young lady holding a bible in her outstretched hand. McKie & Thomson launched her in 1895 and she was lost in 1896. (G. E. Langmuir)*

34. *(Left). In one of the pages in A. P. Elder's scrapbook is a photograph of a figurehead of the young Queen Victoria and this also appears in sketch form. No name or date is given. (Courtesy National Maritime Museum)*

base is a trade label which reads: "Farrington's. Ship and House carvers, cabinet makers, joiners, looking glass and picture frame manufacturers and gilders in general."

Only one reference has been located of Richard Farrington's work for a shipyard and this is a small job for H. S. Edwards of South Shields for "Gilt work for No.2. *Elizabeth 248/31*, £1.8.0."

Fisken.   The name Fisken does not appear in a Trades Directory but in the ledgers of the Laing Yard at Sunderland payments are recorded for carved work carried out by Fisken on *Caledonia 1456/70*, £32.9.0, and on *Bahia 1949/71* and *Teviot 1946/71* totalling £26.2.0

John Folds, Liverpool.   John Folds was working as ship carver in Liverpool from at least 1766 and was joined by his son in about 1790. The day books of Brockbank, shipbuilders, Glasson Dock, Lancaster contain several entries between 1788 and 1799. John Folds cut the carved work for *Wildman 415/99*, including the family crest for the stern, "Or on a pale azure, three bezants Crest out of a mural crown dr. a demi lion issuant proper holding a battleaxe or headed if the first." The other figureheads specifically mentioned are for *Europa* of 1794 and *Betsey 183/1792*. For *Betsey* the carver was paid £30.0.0, while for carved work for an un-named vessel launched in 1797 he received £45.0.0.

John Fraser, Aberdeen.   There is no evidence that John Fraser actually carved figureheads but his name appears four times in the cost books of the Hall yard at Aberdeen. As a carver for *Graphic 1029/72*, £22.16.3. As a carver and gilder for *Juan de la Vega 172/71*, £1.19.0. As a gilder for *Commissary 899/68*, £25.0.0. and *Caliph 963/69*, £35.3.0.

By 1881 he was employing one man and a boy in his workshop.

James Garvie, Aberdeen.   James Garvie, carver, of Aberdeen worked on ships in the yard of Alexander Hall between 1885 and 1890. The work does not appear to have included the carving of figureheads and his efforts ranged from carving the steering gear cover for *Rosalind 365/85* for £1.11.1, carving and decorating panels on *Yallaroi 1565/85* for £4.17.6. to *Jaboatao 653/90* for which he executed carved and decorated work worth £65.3.1.

Grinling Gibbons, London.   Grinling Gibbons was born in Holland of English parents. The family returned to England, first to Yorkshire, then to London where they settled in Deptford, then a centre of shipbuilding. Gibbons was a wood carver by trade and for a time he worked as a ship and architectural carver. It was not long before his talent was recognised and he rose to become the King's Master carver. Gibbons is credited with the carving of the "Golden Cherubs" figurehead which can be seen aboard the *Cutty Sark*.

Gibbs. (David Gibb, London).   In 1890 the ketch *Sunshine 133/90* was built at Whitstable and fitted with a figurehead carved by Gibbs for £2.10.0. Ramage & Ferguson of Leith launched the steam yacht *Iolanda 1647/08* and Gibbs was commissioned to carve the figurehead. One source says that it was removed after being damaged in a collision while another says that it was because of dry rot. Whatever the cause, in 1931 a new figurehead was carved by a Mr. Meadows of Shirley near Birmingham but never fitted. The original is in Seattle, the copy in Mystic Seaport Museum. (*Iolanda* was designed by London based naval architects.)
        The most obvious carver was David Gibb of London who worked in Blackwall from about 1878 to 1913. In 1889 Gibb carved a small figurehead for a clipper bowed Thames pleasure launch *Viscountess Bury*.

Grayfoot & Overton, London.   In 1801 and 1803 when the East Indiaman *Arniston 1433/94* completed her round voyages to China, John Grayfoot carried out repairs to her carved work. In the early 19th. century the Dudman family had a shipyard at Deptford where they built a number of East Indiamen. Account books have survived from 1812 to 1815 which record frequent payments to Grayfoot & Overton varying from £21.10.5 to £87.1.7. Only the name of one vessel is entered, that of *Indus*, a 3rd. rate 74 gun frigate. More information about Grayfoot & Overton is given under "naval carvers."

Robert Hall, London.   The name of Robert Hall is entered in the old directories from 1842 to 1872, but he was already providing carved work for the Admiralty in 1832. The only full record of the work which he carried out for a commercial shipyard is that of Alexander Hall of Aberdeen who were sending him orders for figureheads and carved work from 1838 to 1873. This shipyard placed a lot of orders with London carvers until the local craftsmen became established. Surprisingly enough only 9 out of the 50 ships for which he executed work were actually for owners in London. The remainder were bound for ports as far apart as Wick and Dartmouth. They ranged in size from the schooner *Falcon 85/38* for which he carved a falcon's head for £3.10.0, to the famous *Caliph 963/69* with a demi-female figure, which brought him in £32.10.0. *Caliph* was the most expensive contract which he fulfilled for the Hall yard. Incidentally, the gilder John Fraser who worked on *Caliph* received £35.3.0 for his efforts, while another carver George Wishart was paid £8.15.0. Other tea clippers for which he provided figureheads were *Chrysolite 564/51* at a cost of £9.0.0 and *Cairngorm 938/53* which netted him £21.15.0. When Pitcher on the Thames built *Orinoco 2318/52* Robert Hall "sculpted a spirited and charcteristic figurehead" for her.   Robert Hall cut carved work for other shipyards well away from London. 1841 found Joseph White of East Cowes, Isle of Wight in financial trouble owing £8.0.0. In 1857 Thomas White (The Younger) who had shipyards in

35. *Hall's sketch for*
Sultana 243/68.

financial trouble owing £8.0.0. In 1857 Thomas White (The Younger) who had shipyards in Portsmouth and Gosport closed down with Robert Hall requesting payment for a bill of £5.15.0.

Among items in the records of the Fellows shipbuilding yard at Great Yarmouth is an envelope dated 18th. June 1868 from Robert Hall containing sketches for two figureheads, one for *Sultana 243/68* (35) and the other marked *Sultan*.

Robert Hall's figures were approved by the Admiralty and his work on warships is described under "Naval Carvers".

The Hammonds of Liverpool.   Nothing has turned up about the work of the Hammond family of Liverpool, but over a long period the Trades Directories recorded their names under the heading of "Ship Carver".

Joseph Hammond	1837
John & Henry Hammond	1843-1846
John H. Hammond	1852-1869
Thomas Hammond	1860
John Hoar Hammond and Joseph Pim Hammond	1870-1895

A paragraph in a Liverpool paper stated that the Hammonds had a workshop in Mann Island leading down to Albert Dock where they carved for Whitehaven ships.

George D. Handy, Sunderland.   In the directories and census records Handy is described variously as a "Carver and Gilder", a "Wood Carver and Gilder", and a "Carver, Gilder, and Picture Frame Maker". The Short Bros. Sunderland ledgers show that George Handy worked on five of their vessels in 1872 and on one in 1880. The details of the work are not given, being entered solely as "carving and gilding". For *Regalia 941/72* and *Emerald 934/72* he received £21.5.0 each, and for *Ennerderdale 1250/72*, £41.17.0.

Archibald and John Harriott, North Shields.   There were two Harriott brothers, Archibald and John, both carvers, who set up business as ship carvers in 1828. In 1834 they moved to a larger premises, announcing the change of address with an advertisement in the local paper. The 1841 census shows Archibald as a " carver ", while John is described as an " artist ". It is understood that John went his own way in 1840 leaving Archibald to carry on the carving and gilding business but for a time the whole title of A. & J. Harriott was retained. In 1843 there was another change of address from Tyne Street to Bell Street and an auction was held. It is evident from the list of items for sale that not all figureheads were created to suit the vessel on which they were fitted as the stock in trade included "several Carved Male and Female Busts and Figureheads for Ships of various sizes.

A quantity of Stars, Drops, Brackets, and Lions' Faces for Ships' Sterns and Catheads." After the move to Bell Street another advertisement was inserted in the papers. By 1847 the title of the workshop had been altered simply to Archibald Harriott, and this was the last time that the name appeared. As was common in those days spelling was somewhat slack and the name appears as Harriot, Harriott and Harriat.

The records of H. S. Edwards, Shipbuilders, South Shields show that the Harriotts cut carved work for them on at least seven vessels between 1836 and 1840. The wood used for the figureheads was American Fir @ 1/8 per cu. ft. and the figures were generally small, using 9 cu. ft. each giving figureheads for *Mary Muir 357/39* for £11.10.0 and *Caroline 309/40*, £11.5.0, prices which probably included all the other carved work. *Janet 298/38* had a larger figurehead requiring 16 cu. ft. but the carver only received £6.0.0.

J. & J. Hay and Hay & Lyall, Aberdeen. The name Hay occurs in the directories from 1821 to 1874. That of J. Hay is recorded from 1821 to 1844 where he is described as a "carver, gilder, and instrument maker". By 1850 a partnership had been formed of James & John Hay and they were the carvers for the clipper ship *Stornoway 595/50* for which they cut a male figurehead and did gilding for a total of £17.0.0. Other work on *Stornoway* was carried out by George Hellyer from London. By 1866 another partnership had been created, that of Hay & Lyall and they were engaged in work for the Hall yard for the next twenty years. The entries in the cost books are not always detailed but they give the impression that in the main Hay & Lyall's contribution was general carving and gilding. Nevertheless this secondary work brought in a good income. The famous *Sobraon 2130/66* was worth £31.0.0 to them while the main carver was paid £66.9.0. From *Douglas 873/66* they did even better, netting £170.0.0, while the other two carvers and gilders received only £45.11.0 between them. At the bottom of the scale came *Elissa 431/77* for which they received only £3.6.0. out of a total of £18.4.4. In all Hay & Lyall worked on 23 vessels for Hall.

Peter Hay, Greenock. Old cash books from the yard of Scott's of Greenock record that in 1803 they paid Peter Hay £5.13.0 for furnishing two badges for Captain Beatson for the revenue cutter *Prince William*.

William Hector, Aberdeen. William Hector was engaged in work for Alexander Hall for only a short time from 1883 to 1885. It is evident that he was only a minor carver and was cutting the secondary decorative carvings. Six of his jobs were for small steamships which paid him from £1.4.0. for *Deeside 592/83* to £16.15.6. for *Glentanar 1595/84*. Others were for sailing ships ranging from *Yallaroi 1565/88* for which he carved the stern for £11.6.0, to *Rosalind 365/85* on which he worked on the steering gear cover for £1.2.0. *Rosalind* was simply decorated with a total bill of only £14.3.1.

Ralph Hedley, Newcastle. Ralph Hedley was born in 1848 in Richmond, Yorkshire and was apprenticed as a boy to Mr. Tweedy, a wood carver. He founded his own wood carving business in 1869 in company with James Wishart. Two years later Wishart died and Ralph Hedley carried on as an "artistic and architectural wood carver." Over the years he provided a great deal of carved work for ships built on the banks of the Tyne though the word 'figurehead' is not mentioned. He carved for Wigham, Richardson from 1882, two early jobs being a "Neptune" for £7.12.6, and carved work for £30.12.6. Contracts for liners from Swan, Hunter were profitable. *Lawang* of 1891 brought him £240.8.6, while *Aoranga* of 1897 was worth £137.8.6. In 1894 he received orders from Hawthorn, Leslie for mouldings and an eagle's head for £12.0.0., and a repeat order, this time worth £25.0.0. Brackets and mouldings for Scotswood Shipbuilding Co. in 1892 fetched in £201.17 6. He carved for ships from the Laing yard including *Westralia 2884/96* which was worth £104.10.0. Some tracery panels for the Mitchell shipyard in 1885 were priced at £6.0.0.

Ralph Hedley was also an outstanding artist and it is for this that he is best known. When he died he left behind many sketch books but none of the sketches show his carved work.

The Hellyer Family (38).   The name Hellyer is the best known of the figurehead carvers mainly because it was a Hellyer who carved the figureheads of *Warrior* and *Cutty Sark*. Their activities go back nearly 400 years but they do not appear as ship carvers until 1799 when they began to do work for the Admiralty. They originated in the Southampton area, and established themselves at Cosham, later opening branches in London and Newcastle. No shipyard records have survived of their work for London yards but fortunately we have information from other sources. One item only was reported in the press. In 1850 Robinson & Russell of Millwall built a schooner yacht called *Titania* with a bust of the Fairy Queen herself as a figurehead, modelled by the eminent sculptor James Bell and carved by one of the Hellyer family. In an entry in the Admiralty letter books it is recorded that the Hellyers "worked well" with Richard & Henry Green, shipbuilders. Alexander Hall of Aberdeen sent orders to Hellyer and Browning in 1837 and 1840 to cut figureheads for five smallish vessels. *Orlando 157/37* and *Commodore 149/37* had "male busts" for which Hall's paid them £3.13.6 each, while *Catherine 246/37* and *Ythan 84/37* had "female busts" which cost £4.10.0 and £3.7.6. No other carved work was fitted on the ships. In 1850/51 George Hellyer went up to Aberdeen and lodged there while carving for the tea clipper *Stornoway 595/50* and *John Taylor 787/51*. For *Stornoway* Hellyer was responsible only for the secondary carving worth £5.10.0, while J. & J. Hay included the figurehead in their bill of £17.0.0. The figurehead of *John Taylor* was Hellyer's work and cost £10.0.0. In 1858, after he had returned to London, he cut the figurehead for another tea clipper, *Ziba 497/58*. He was paid £10.10.0 for his efforts, but the vessel must have been very plain as the remaining carving work was done by George Wishart and George Hughes, adding a mere £7.9.8 to her cost. In 1869 George Hellyer was on the move once more, this time to Glasgow, where he took up residence in a block maker's shop in Govan. In all the books dealing with *Cutty Sark* credit for the carving of the figurehead is given to Frederick Hellyer which leaves us wondering what George Hellyer was doing in Glasgow. Did he in fact carve the figurehead of *Cutty Sark* under the eagle eye of Captain George Moodie who was overseeing the construction of the vessel or was he merely executing the decorative carving ? While he was up there he completed a small job for Scott's of Bowling valued at £6.0.0. Later Scotts of Greenock sent down to London for carved work for *Nestor 2100/80*, a small contract worth £11.7.6.

Hellyer Bros., who were Arthur Henry Hellyer and James Edward Hellyer, established a branch in South Shields in 1867, and this was commemorated in 1884 with a paragraph in the book describing local businesses(39). Included in their patrons were Readhead & Sons, Ltd, who gave them orders over the years 1876 to 1901 worth a steady £150 per annum. Between 1872 and 1884 the Laing yard placed orders for carved work the most expensive being for the steamship *Estaban*

38. This dog figurehead came from the schooner yacht Gelert 166/67 *and represents the favourite deer hound of Dr. Parkes. On the back of the photograph is the inscription "By James Hellyer, carver to the Royal Navy."*
(Courtesy Mrs. Ruth Smith, U.S.A.)

Hellyer Brothers, Ship and Ornamental Carvers, Fowler Street, South Shields.—The firm of Messrs. Hellyer Brothers is at once one of the oldest and most celebrated in existence in connection with all classes of ornamental and decorative carving ; and the name of Hellyer, always closely associated with this artistic handicraft, can be distinctly traced back for upwards of three hundred years. The present headquarters in South Shields were opened seventeen years ago by the present sole head and proprietor of the house, who represents the seventh generation of the Hellyer family in the business which has brought the name such universal celebrity. The original firm was established in Portsmouth, where the founder held an official appointment by diploma. Another branch of the family (father and brother of the South Shields principal) now do Government work in London. At South Shields the firm carry on a most extensive and high-class business in ornamental ship carving ; and one of their greatest achievements in this special line has recently been accomplished, and consists in the execution of all the carving and decorative work incidental to the great ironclad *Victoria*, a triumph of Tyneside industry in the building and equipment of war-ships, which was recently launched from the yard of Sir W. G. Armstrong, Mitchell & Co., Limited. We understand an ancestor of the Messrs. Hellyer also did the carving on Nelson's famous flag-ship the *Victory*. Messrs. Hellyer are at present engaged upon the cabin carvings (of the most elaborate and *recherché* character) for the steamship *Alphonso XII.*, now being completed on the Tyne, and which will be one of the finest finished and largest steamers ever built on this river. These two citations serve to indicate the class of work of which Messrs. Hellyer are capable ; and it is beyond all question that this house has no superior in the United Kingdom in the execution of carvings and wood decorations for ships of every description. In church and house work the firm are also noted in a more than ordinary degree, and they carry on an extensive picture-frame business ; whilst within the last five years Mr. Hellyer has developed another notable department, the actual buying and selling of pictures themselves. During the year 1858 Mr. Hellyer inaugurated an excellent show of pictures at his premises in Fowler Street, South Shields, the admission to which was free to the public ; and this he intends to be the first of an annual series of similar exhibitions, which promise to meet with ready appreciation. The whole establishment of this firm in Fowler Street (an extensive and commodious three-storey block of premises, with spacious basement workrooms), is pervaded with an artistic atmosphere ; and the present policy of Mr. Hellyer justifies the assumption that the place will in the near future become a centre of pictorial and decorative art which cannot fail to add greatly to the reputation of his noted house.

de Antunano 1804/84 for which they were paid £21.6.4, compared with the £77.4.0. which Joseph Melvin received for his share. Arthur Hellyer began working with his father in 1866 at the age of 14 in a workshop in the Wigram yard on the Thames and he later spent 30 years on the Tyne where the Hellyers did most of the carved work for the Armstrong yards. When *City of Rome 8144/81* was launched at the Naval Armaments yard in Barrow it bore carved work which had occupied Arthur Hellyer there for 8 months while he cut "the magnificent figure of Julius Caesar with flowing robes running 50 ft. along the bow, together with the internal carvings." (40)

When William Parmiter, Shipbuilder, of Gosport and Southampton went bankrupt in 1832 he owed James Edward Hellyer of Cosham £12.12.0. Another bankrupt shipyard, that of Frederick Preston of Little Yarmouth (near Great Yarmouth), failed in 1840 and was in debt to William Browning and his partner James Edward Hellyer of Rotherhithe for £29.18.0. In Cosham James E. Hellyer and James Hellyer were in partnership as Jas. E. & Jas. Hellyer from about 1847. J. Samuel White's ledgers have a number of entries against "Hellyer, carver" from 1880 to 1892, but few of the entries are detailed. *"Bird*-eagle head, £1.15.0", "*Grey Witch 18/82*, two badges, £2.15.0." One other mercantile figurehead which we know was carved by the Hellyers was that of *British Queen 145/38* of Glasgow. In 1849 she was in collision with *H.M.S. Sphinx* and lost her figurehead and this was replaced at the Admiralty's expense for £4.15.0.

William Hepburn, Newcastle. The name of William Hepburn, "ship carver" appears in the trades directories between 1850 and 1879, save that in 1875 the title was Hepburn & Irwin.

Joseph Hodgson, Sunderland. Joseph Hodgson carved a couple of figureheads for James Laing, *Ayres Quay 92/52* for only £2.0.0. and *Jane* for a slightly dearer £4.10.0. Four other orders which followed in 1854 were recorded as "steering wheel" at prices which ranged from £2.10.0. to £4.10.0, which must have included the carving on the steering wheel cover. The records of the Doxford yard show that he carved figureheads for them in 1855 and 1856 for two ships. He may

40. *(Above). Arthur Hellyer spent eight months in Barrow working on this figurehead and trail boards for* City of Rome *8144/81 which stretched 50 feet along the stem.*

40. *(Left). When J. & G. Thomson launched* Claymore *760/81 the carvers on their books were William Houston and M. & J. Allan. It was common to see Clyde steamers with figureheads. He is shown as he was before rescue and repair by the Scottish Fisheries Museum.*

have moved to London where a Joseph Hodgson made entries in the directories from 1867 to 1883.

    Henry Hopkins, London.   Thanks to very early letter books preserved by Scotts of Greenock we have some knowledge of the work of Henry Hopkins of London. In 1798 they wrote to him-"We wish you to make us a fashionable lady head in the present taste, five feet long and send it by the first Berwick smack to Leith." (*Diana 800/98*). They were in touch with him again in 1803. *Pitt 307/99* a ship built in Ulverston had been brought in for overhaul and despite her being only four years old she was in need of a new figurehead. "We wrote to you some time ago that we wanted you to cut a head for a ship about 300 tons called *Pitt*. The owners are very desirous to have the likeness of Mr. Pitt as near as possible. We are informed that no carver in London can execute so well as you. We request that you will write to us on receipt of this and make a pencil sketch on one side of the letter and as he is now a military character we suppose you will dress him in uniform. P. S. We leave the design to you." (The figurehead cost them £13.6.6.). When they approached Mr. Hopkins again in 1818 they were more specific in their requirements :"We, having your favour of the 22nd. July, the sketch of the Malay was not made to scale but merely fancy, done in a very hurried way and by no means correct. We cannot without the Figure give a sketch of the trail boards but they are of no consequence and you may just send the Head without them. The Figure will be about 8 ft. projection from the hooding and the cheeks spaced on the knee about 10 inches asunder with a fine swinging Rail. We wish to make this a very warlike Turkish or Malay figure. Mr. Sinclair will probably wait upon you with a drawing of the proper costume. The drapery must be flowing and easy and the whole finished in the very best style to give effect in setting the Head." (*Malay 215/18*).

    Henry Hopkins seems to have had quite a reputation. In 1807 Benjamin Tanner of Dartmouth went into receivership and among his creditors was Mr. Hopkins with a bill for £87.15.0. The shipyard must have been a busy one as the legal papers mention seven vessels just completed or on the stocks, as well as six 18 gun brigs for the Royal Navy for which the Admiralty still owed Tanner considerable sums of money. These included *Wolf* of 1804 and *Ferret* of 1806.

    Henry Hopkins had his name in the directories from 1798 to 1824.

William Houston, Glasgow.   There were Houstons in the carving and gilding business in Glasgow for many years. In 1839 it was A & W. Houston, in 1855 the company became W. A. & W. Houston and around 1860, simply W. Houston. The 1861 census describes William Houston as a master carver employing 8 men and 9 boys.

In the shipyard records it is only the name of William Houston which appears. A couple of small jobs for Denny of Dumbarton in 1847 and 1848 were a beginning. *Lochfyne 83/47*, "carving name boards" at £1.16.0. and *Secret 311/48*, "carved work" at £16.0.0. In a newspaper the report of the launch of *Ivanhoe 1034/53* from the yard of A. McMillan states that "the figurehead representing Sir Walter Scott's Ivanhoe was carved by A. & W. Houston of Glasgow." The records of J. & G. Thomson of Clydebank show that they employed William Houston on an almost continuous basis from at least 1857 to 1883 (41). Only five vessels are named against payments, *Agia Sophia 1437/57, Havelock 629/58, Heather Bell 152/58, Giraffe 677/60* and *Cortes* of 1862. The last was a good contract for which he received £64.10.0. On most of these vessels Houston shared the carved work with others. Other entries in the cash books show how variable business could be. 1857 brought in £215.4.8, 1867 only £11.12.0, and 1881, £437.3.4. Houston also provided carved work for the small shipyard of D. & A. Fullerton in Ayr which ceased building in 1860.

John Hudson, Port St. Mary, I. O. M.   There is preserved in the Isle of Man a rather badly decayed figurehead from the schooner *Spray 60/77*. The carving is reputed to have been carried out by John Hudson.

David Hughes, Liverpool.   David Hughes occupied a workshop at the foot of Bridgewater Street, down by the docks. For many years he carved figureheads and ornamental work for warships and merchant ships built at Laird's yard in Birkenhead, among them the steam yacht *Portia 432/06*. One of the largest figureheads on which he worked was 19 ft. overall, for the bows of *Waesland 4856/67*(41). She had been built by J. & G. Thomson of Clydebank as the Cunard liner *Russia* and when she lost her figurehead in a collision Mr. Hughes was asked to carve the replacement, a figure representing Russia with a crown on her head and a cross at her neck. He is credited with carving the figurehead for *Carib Prince 2048/93*, built in Sunderland by Short Bros.

David Hughes emigrated to the United States where he became professor of carving at an American university.

41. Chaa-Sze 556/60 *came from Alexander Hall's yard in Aberdeen. The name means ' Tea Taster' and the carver George Hughes has portrayed various aspects of the tea trade. (Sketch by Richard Hunter)*

41. *This sketch shows the replacement figurehead for* Waesland 4856/67 *which was carved by David Hughes. (Sketch by R. Hunter)*

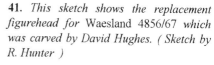

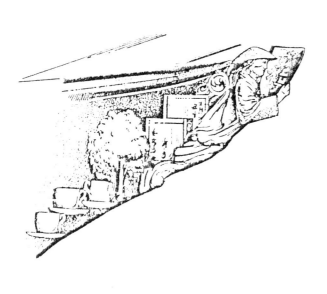

George Hughes, Aberdeen.   In the 1861 census George Hughes was called a "master wood carver, aged 32, born in England, employing one apprentice. "He worked on contracts for Alexander Hall from 1853 to 1889 and during this period he was involved on some 80 vessels, in many cases sharing the carved work with others. At first he was only given the general carved work to do but from 1862 he was executing bow carvings for every vessel on which he worked. Out of 30 heads which he carved between 1861 and 1868, 15 were described as "shields ". He cut figureheads for several tea clippers including *Friar Tuck 662/57* (43), for which he was paid £24.0.0, with George Wishart receiving £8.0.0, and Kerr & Bowman doing the gilding for £5.6.6. Apart from the usual human forms Hughes carved a number of animal heads. *Martinet 73/56* had a dog for £6.10.0, *Yang-Tze 688/63*, a dragon for £13.10.0, *Sobraon 2130/66*, a lion for £66.9.0. (a price which included all the carved work), and the whaler *Eclipse 434/67* an eagle for £12.0.0. George Hughes also provided carved work for small shipyards such as Francis Robertson of Peterhead, which, when they ceased trading in 1868 owed Hughes £3.10.0 for a figurehead for their last ship. Another was Leckie, Wood & Munro of Torry, opposite Aberdeen, who went out of business in 1870 owing Hughes 14/6 for carved work.

Joseph Humphries, Greenock.   Joseph Humphries put entries in the directories from 1873 to 1907. The earliest contract found was a single job for Russells of Port Glasgow when he carved the stern for *Easdale 100/76* for £2.15.0. He had more luck with Scotts of Greenock, as the yard sent him orders regularly from 1880 to 1895. The entries in the cash books do not detail the work done but as most of them only have his name against them we can assume that Humphries carved the figurehead where one was fitted. The contracts varied from 1/6 for *Malange 3544/90* to £45.18.8 for *Santanna 342/87*. The carvings on the paddle boxes for *Marchioness of Breadalbane 246/90* cost £3.1.0. In all he provided carved work for 37 of Scott's ships.

Hutton of Dundee. (64).   One of the local shipping records in Dundee states that Hutton was famed for his figureheads in the 1850s, while another credits Hutton with several between 1841 and 1852. There were three ship carvers named Hutton in Dundee who carried out contracts for local shipyards. Andrew, who was working in Dock street in 1845 and who died in 1851, and his two sons, James born in 1832, and Andrew, born in 1842. Thus it would appear that it was Andrew senior who carved the figurehead for *Robin Gray 292/41*, built by Thomas Adamson, depicting a robin, and *Tay 608/50* , launched by Calman & Martin, having on her bow "a full length Mary Queen of Scots with Darnley and Rizzio on the stern with a Scottish lion in the centre." His son James was probably responsible for the figureheads on *George and Lucy 220/51*, built by John Brown of Dundee, using a double head depicting the owner's two children, and also *Harriette 328/52* from Calman & Martin's yard and *Harkaway 899/52* built in Dundee by Alexander Stephen. In 1852 Andrew Hutton cut the carved work for *Eleanor Dodson 303/52* built by J. & A. Calman, a bust for £7.10.0 and trail boards for 10/-. William Anderson who had a shipyard at Arbroath, just up the coast, had carved work cut by Andrew Hutton in about 1850. The two brothers worked together in a workshop in King William Dock until 1862 after which there are no more entries in the directories.

Andrew Hutton, Glasgow.   In 1851 Alexander Stephen established a shipyard at Kelvinhaugh, Glasgow and shortly afterwards took on to their payroll Andrew Hutton to be their carver for an agreed period of five years. In February 1856 Hutton requested permission to leave their employ to enter into business on his own account with a year and a half of the contract still to run. The Stephens cancelled his contract without penalty but extracted a condition that "they would receive what carving they might require within that time at a reasonable rate." It would be Andrew Hutton who carved the figurehead of *Hurricane 1111/53* which, when Messrs. Stephen launched her, was sufficiently striking as to impel the newspaper reporter to write: " It is one of the finest figureheads we have seen. We presume the good-looking he-deity is intended to represent the Spirit of the Storm with his locks blown back and his 'eye in a fine frenzy rolling'. We were struck by the elaborate and careful carving of the whole figure, which would have done credit to the atelier of a sculptor, and very different indeed from the ordinary run of figureheads. It was sculpted by one of Messrs. Stephen and Sons' workmen, and deserves more than a mere passing encomium."

Hutton also executed carved work for the Clydebank yard of J. & G. Thompson during the period 1856 to 1860. Most of the entries in the cash books do not give the name of the vessel but during that period Hutton was paid: 1856 (£24.0.0), 1857 (£88.6.0 which included *Agia Sophia 1437/57*, the only vessel named), 1858 (£37.6.0), 1859 (£8.0.0), 1860 (£8.0.0). An old voucher book from the yard of J. R. Napier has survived and contains a hand-written invoice from Andrew Hutton for £21.7.0 for carving bow ornaments, stern carving, eagles on the paddle boxes and name boards for the paddle steamer *Admiral 586/58* for Riga. Hutton was purely a carver and the gilding for this vessel was done by "a house & ship painter & gilder."

James Hutton, Sunderland.   There were entries in the Trades Directories under James Hutton from 1865 until 1894 under the heading of "ship carver". In 1880 his name appears in the record books of Short Bros. shipyard and between 1880 and 1884 he provided carved work for no less than 53 steamships. In those days many steamers had figureheads and even if they did not, they still carried considerable decorative work on the bow and round the stern. Costs ranged from as little as £1.0.0. for *Bellini 1730/80* to £42.16.6. for *St. Pauli* of 1881.

John Johnson, North Shields.
John Johnson put an advertisement in Ward's Directory in 1854 announcing himself as a "ship carver" and entries were made until at least 1865. There had been a

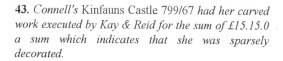

JOHN JOHNSON,
HOUSE AND SHIP CARVER AND GILDER,
23, Camden Street, North Shields.
☞ *Chimney Looking Glass and Picture Frame Manufacturer.*

single entry under that name in 1844 and between 1847 and 1867 there were entries under Francis Johnson (House and Ship Carver) who worked at a different address.

43. *The elegant figure cut by George Hughes for the tea clipper* Friar Tuck 662/57 *is handsomely carved but does not portray the portly cleric of the Robin Hood legends. The vessel was built by Hall of Aberdeen and was wrecked in the Scilly Is. in 1863 (Tresco Valhalla)*

43. Connell's Kinfauns Castle 799/67 *had her carved work executed by Kay & Reid for the sum of £15.15.0 a sum which indicates that she was sparsely decorated.*

Thomas Kay, Dumbarton and Glasgow.   Thomas Kay was a well-known ship carver who worked first in Dumbarton and from 1820 in Glasgow until his death in 1852.

He carried out a number of contracts for the Denny shipyards in Dumbarton between 1834 and 1852, 30 of which are detailed in the company cost records. Some of the early ones itemised the decorative work which he provided:

Sept. 1845 to Thomas Kay, carving for *Loch Lomond 95/44*. No.45. Denny & Rankine.

Headboard	£2.10.0	Carving 300 ???? on ceiling @ 4¼d	£5. 6.3
Quarters	3. 3.0	Wood	2/4
Stern	3. 5.0	Men putting up same	15.9
Companion and name boards	16/0	Stern panels	2.12.0
Four oak sofa elbows	3 16.0	Carving 8 oak pateras	4/6
Polishing --do--	7/6	Carving 6 fir clasps	9/0
Wood	3/2	Glass frame and plate	1.14.0

Total £30.0.6.

Ship. No.47, *Sylphide 182/47* was a profitable one for Kay as the bill came to a total of £220.4.4. At the other end of the scale was the schooner *Shamrock 141/49* which only netted him £4.15.0.

After the death of Thomas Kay his foreman Thomas Shanks became a partner in the business with his widow and the name of Kay & Shanks was adopted. When he died he was one of the few carvers to be honoured with an obituary.

THE LATE MR THOMAS KAY.—Many of our readers in this neighbourhood will observe, with regret, the demise of this much respected and truly talented individual, whose eminent designs, and executions in ship-carving, were the admiration of the shipbuilders in this quarter and elsewhere, and whose many other qualities will not soon be forgotten by those who were favoured with his acquaintanceship. As a man, a tradesman, and a friend, he was universally esteemed, and his death has left a blank in many a circle that will not soon be filled up.

Kay & Shanks, Glasgow.   After Thomas Shanks became a partner with Kay's widow to form the new firm of Kay & Shanks, Denny of Dumbarton continued to send them orders. The partnership lasted until 1857 when Shanks departed to set up his own ship carving business. During the short period of their existence they received some very remunerative contracts from Denny's. *Indian 1765/54* cost £200.9.6, *Canadian 1765/54* brought in £219.5.4, and *Andes 1440/52* and *Alps 1440/52* netted £794.77.6 between them. Even the lowest figure of £61.1.0 for the steamer *Falcon 477/54* was still an expensive contract for that time.

Only on two occasions were the company's efforts reported in the newspapers but on both occasions the reporter was more interested in the interior. For *Marie Stewart 563/56* they commented that: "The feature of the carvings and decorations generally is that, while they are rich and elegant, they all bear proofs of design, and are entirely free from the all too common fault of profusion and overcrowding. Mr. Shanks of Glasgow under whose personal charge they were executed, has certainly gained great credit by his efforts in this department." When *North American. 1675/56* went on her trial trip they reported that "The grotesque carvings by Messrs.Kay & Shanks are in their own way unsurpassed."

Kay & Reid, Glasgow.   Following the departure of Thomas Shanks in 1857 the name of Kay & Shanks was replaced by Kay & Reid. Kay's widow was still alive and the new partner was James G. Reid. Under his influence the workshop expanded from 5 men and 5 boys in 1861 to 35 boys by 1871. as their advertisement shows, ship carving was only a small part of their business (45).

When Thomas Shanks left the firm he did not take away all the Denny 'goodwill' and Kay & Reid received many profitable orders from Dumbarton over the years which followed. *Principe Alfonso 1927/63*, £383.17.0, *Infanta Isobel 1933/63*, £392.0.0, and *A. Lopez 1969/65*, £893.3.0, an immense expenditure in those days for decorative work. Even two tugs launched in 1864 had £50.11.0 spent between them on carved work. Very seldom did an order fall below £100.0.0.

They received orders from Elder of Govan. Unfortunately the cost books do not give names before 1873 in which year Kay & Reid cut carved work for *Potosi 4219/73*, £45.0.0 for labour, £35.9.1 for wood. In 1878 they executed carved work for six small gunboats, the first of which was

H.M.S.Comus 2380/78, each of whose carved work cost around £60.0.0. Elder's customers were not so free with their money as those of Denny, and Kay & Reid generally were paid less than £45.0.0. for their efforts. Two of the ships which cost just this were *Liguria 4666/74* and *Iberia 4671/73.* Over the period 1865 to 1878 Charles Connell placed orders including the carved work for the tea clipper *Spindrift 899/67* for £17.15.0. Connell's customers too, were quite close fisted and even for the much vaunted China Clippers Kay & Reid were paid but small amounts. Take *Taymouth Castle 627/65* for which they were paid £15.11.0. Quite a number of letters between Charles Connell and Kay & Reid have been saved and these show that even on a small steamer quite a lot of internal decorative work was required, *City of Agra 3273/79.*

Egg and dart cornice moulding	2/2 per foot.
Picture frame moulding	1/8 per foot
Veined cornice moulding	10d. per foot.
Large capitals	7/- each.
Small capitals	5/6 each.
Trusses	7/- each.
Mahogany table standards	1/9 each
Carved and gilded mirror, clock case, plate 60" x 30"	£7. 5.0.
Carved and gilded mirrors, plates 50" x 30"	£5.12.0.

Customers could be awkward. Kay & Reid had only just completed the name boards and stern decoration with the coat of arms of Liverpool for *City of Liverpool,* Ship No.125 in 1881, when Connell's announced the owners' decision to change the vessel's name to *City of Calcutta 3919/81* and requested the carvers to supply a new set of name boards and a new shield for the stern. It was Connell's practice to issue a 'carving sketch' to be returned, filled in, for approval. On one occasion the sketch was sent back to Kay & Reid with the comment "Your sketch is not clear and we can make nothing of it." Many Connell ships carried only a figurehead, "No.130-neither stern carving nor trail boards are needed on this vessel". (*Vanduara 2086/82*).

Robert Duncan of Port Glasgow placed three orders with Kay & Reid in 1867/8, the first being *Helen Burns 799/67* worth £42.18.11, but another yard in the area, Russell & Co., went to them for 15 of their earlier ships in the years between 1876 and 1879 before changing their allegiance to local carvers. A typical Russell order was that of *Anglo-Norman 822/76,* Ship No.4:

Figurehead, trailboards, stern, figures on quarters, shield on stern all for	£13.10.0.
Carving and gilding 112 ft. of cornice moulding for saloon	7.18.8.
Ornamental capitals	6. 0.0.

The original order for *Falls of Clyde 1809/79,* Ship No.17, which is still afloat was billed by Kay & Reid for:

To exterior and interior carving and gilt work, one figurehead, trailboards, circular stern, also carving and two finishes for the poop	£15. 0.0
Carving and gilding 84 ft. cornice moulding @ 1/2 per ft.	4.18.0.
Carving and gilding 16 capitals @ 7/6 each.	6. 0.0.

Kay & Reid's masterpiece was the figurehead for the ironclad *H.M.S. Black Prince 9210/61* (97) ,built by Robert Napier, which was hewn from a built-up block of timber 16 ft.long, made up of smaller pieces dowelled and glued together. This outstanding figurehead (sadly allowed to decay)

46. *Kay & Reid were the contract carvers for Wm. Denny of Dumbarton when the clipper bowed steamer* Rotomahana 1763/79 *was built.(Courtesy Alexander Turnbull Library, Wellington, New Zealand)*

46. England's Glory 751/69 *was built by Pile of Sunderland whose regular carver was John Lindsay. This is a beautiful example of the figurehead carver's art.*

showed Edward, the Black Prince in a complete suit of armour of the period with a battleaxe in one hand, the other resting on the hilt of his sword. Napier's went to Kay & Reid for at least one other figurehead, that of *Scotia 4050/61*. When they built the small paddle steamer *Victoria 112/58* the drawing showed a plain vessel with little decoration in evidence. However, a letter from Napier to Kay & Reid lists a considerable amount of carved work aboard her.

6 carved seat legs	2 round moulding
42 ft. of carving for seats	4 seat elbows
6 trusses for companion	one drop end for seat
9 seat legs	4 name boards
Top of companion	6 companion seat legs
Turned pineapple for companion	

In an old voucher book from the short lived yard of James R. Napier three invoices are stuck in, one representing considerable minor carved work for the Mersey ferry steamer *Liscard 100/58*, totalling £35.16.0. Another covers the name boards and stern carvings for the steamer *Athanasian 296/60* at a cost of £9.10.0. The third is for the external carved work on an un-named steamer.

The cost books of Ramage & Ferguson of Leith do not give the carver's name. However, by the merest chance one name has turned up. In 1934 the American owner of the steam yacht *Narada* was looking for a replacement figurehead, the old one having been damaged at some time. In the ensuing correspondence it transpired that the original had been carved by Kay & Reid when the vessel had been built as *Semiramis 491/89*. This name crops up several times on ships' bows and refers to the Queen of Assyria, (810-806 B.C.), by legend the daughter of the fish goddess Artigatis. The replacement figurehead, based on Kay & Reid's carving sketch, now resides in the Mariners' Museum at Newport News. The Union Shipbuilding Company of Glasgow was short-lived, constructing only five ships before going bankrupt in 1865 owing Kay & Reid £68.16.6, a sum which would have covered a lot of carved work, probably for the sailing ship *Glenbirnie* which they had just completed. When Laurence Hill of Port Glasgow went into receivership in 1870 they owed £9.19.6. They had recently launched the clippers *Sikh 1200/70* and *Geraldine Paget 1200/70*. James

Reid began bankruptcy proceedings in 1883 though the name of Kay & Reid remained in the directories until 1889. The figurehead of *Semiramis* must have been one of the last to leave their workshop. Kay & Reid must have had a fair amount of business in the yards on the lower reaches of the Clyde as they found it worth while opening a workshop in Greenock between 1865 and 1867.

John Kenwright, Liverpool.   Kenwright's name appears in the directories from 1870 to 1886 but there are no relevant records extant for the Liverpool and Birkenhead shipyards. However a newspaper in the 1920s recalled some of his activities. He is credited with cutting the figurehead for *Sir Henry Havelock 460/62* which portrayed the hero of the Indian Mutiny. He also executed the stern which was carved in medallion style with British flags and laurels on each side with a motto below reading "Providencia Fido". (Trust in Providence). Another paragraph states that Hammond & Kenwright had a large workshop in Mann Island, a street leading down to the Albert Dock, where they carved and renovated figureheads for ships which sailed into Whitehaven. There is no indication in the Trades Directory that Hammond and Kenwright actually worked together as partners.

John G. Kyle, Sunderland.   In the early records of James Laing, Sunderland there are entries against G. Kyle, carver, for *Kelloe 500/66,* £3.8.0, and *Resolute 229/69*, £10.7.0. There then follows a gap of twenty years before the name of Kyle appears again, this time John G. Kyle who carried out work for them on at least 29 ships between 1888 and 1898, all of them steamers. One of these, *Clydesdale 3565/95*, definitely had a figurehead, and despite the fact that she was purely a cargo ship she had a full clipper bow and her carved work was valued at £16.10.0. The most expensive contract was for *Ville de Havre 3165/89* which cost Laing £52.11.3, and *Perou* 3091/90 which earned Kyle £52.16.6. The least expensive was *Tuscarora 6117/98* which cost 2/11.

James Law, Dundee.   James Law born in 1837 came from a family of ship owners and business men and yet around 1860 he became a wood carver and soon made a name for himself in Dundee as "a ship and figurehead carver." He started off in a loft in a small shipyard at the King William Dock, a yard which was taken over by Alexander Stephen & Son of Glasgow. His workshop resembled a museum, full of models of human figures and stuffed animals which he used to guide him as he worked on each figurehead. He carved many figureheads for his landlords the

47. *"In the busy dockland of the 19th. century the services of one specialist were always in demand. James Law (1837-1903) was a wood carver whose figureheads graced many of Dundee's finest sailing ships including whalers and clippers from A. Stephen & Co." (Courtesy A. G. Law)*

47. *James Law has been given credit for carving the figurehead for Lawhill 2749/92 built by W. R. Thomson of Dundee. Several sources have described this as one of the most beautiful ever carved.*

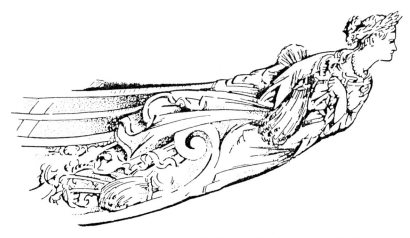

48. *James Law's drawing for the figurehead of* Ceres. *(Courtesy A. G. Law.)*

Stephens, but he also cut them for other Dundee shipyards and for yards elsewhere. His favourite subject was the eagle and when he moved out of his loft to another site in Trades Lane he carved a 6 ft. high eagle and mounted it above the door of his new workshop. Two of his eagles survived for many years, one over the gate of the Eagle Mills which has since disappeared and one over the door of the Eagle Inn in Broughty Ferry, still in situ. Among the Stephen ships for which he cut figureheads were *Lochee 1728/74, Duntrune 1565/75* and *Aurora 580/76.* In 1902 Law carved his last figurehead, that for *Saragossa 2289/02.* A sketch has been preserved which shows a *Ceres,* (48) drawn by James Law, holding a sickle in her left hand while below her right arm is a sheaf of corn. On the trailboards are depicted a variety of agricultural implements. Law did not work alone and in 1861 he was employing 2 men, while by 1871 there were 3 men and 3 boys, one his son David, then aged 10 years who did not follow his father in the carving business. The name of James Law appears in the bankruptcy proceedings of two small shipyards. David Smeaton of Perth owed him £8.2.0 when he closed his yard in 1862 and the Perth New Shipbuilding Company failed in 1867 with a debt of £3.0.0

William Law, Dundee.   Another Law worked as a ship carver in Dundee, William Law, son of a slater. Born in 1852 his name is entered in the directories between 1878 and 1885, though in later issues he is merely called a "wood carver." He did start ship carving at an earlier date. When the yard of J. McPherson of Dundee went into liquidation in 1872 they owed William Law £ 6.0.0.

R. Lee, Liverpool.   There is no record of the activities of R. Lee except for a sketch book in private hands which shows nine suggested designs for figureheads. This page was first printed in the book "Liverpool Ships in the 18th. Century" and is reproduced here by courtesy of Hodder & Stoughton Ltd. Lee emigrated in the early 19th. century to Jersey where he carried on business as a ship, sign and ornamental carver. (48).

48. *Two very contrasting figures from Lee's sketchbook*

Alexander Leslie, Dundee. Born in Dundee in 1844 Alexander Leslie's name first appeared in the Trades Directory in 1867 as a "ship carver." During his working career he described himself variously as a ship carver, a wood carver, a carver and gilder, and a ship and ornamental carver. He died in 1890. One small yard for which he worked was

Roy & Mitchell of Alloa which gave up shipbuilding in 1879 with an outstanding debt to Leslie of £10.5.0. Another yard which failed was Black & Noble of Montrose who closed in 1877 owing Leslie the sum of £8.4.3. This advertisement inserted by Leslie in the local directory is one of the few to be located.

```
┌─────────────────────────────────┐
│   ALEXANDER LESLIE,             │
│  SHIP AND ORNAMENTAL CARVER,    │
│      105  SEAGATE,              │
│           DUNDEE.               │
└─────────────────────────────────┘
```

Arthur Levison, Swansea and Gloucester. Two brothers J. G. & A. Levison, from Sunderland, settled in Swansea where they practiced the art of the ship carver in premises on the North Dock. They carved the figurehead for *Hamlet 253/69* which was modelled by George Melville, a well-known actor of the day. The same gentleman posed later for the figurehead of *Stranger 623/93*, built in Nova Scotia. They also carved the figurehead for a vessel called *Darwin 522/84* which was being built in Prince Edward Island for Swansea owners.

They moved to Gloucester where they continued to work as ship carvers and when one of the brothers died, the other, Arthur, there being little demand for figureheads, went into business as an architectural carver. Nevertheless, he did, from time to time cut a figurehead (2). Arthur Levison executed figureheads for ships built in Portmadoc, one of them was possibly *Isallt 133/09*. An article in Sea Breezes states that he carved the figurehead for *Loch Trool 1367/84* (49). This vessel was built in Glasgow in 1884 but she lost her figurehead in a collision in 1910 and it would be the replacement to which the writer refers.

When *Cutty Sark* was being overhauled in 1955 it was decided that she should have a new figurehead and a search was made for a carver. Arthur Levison's son had helped him as a young man and he was commissioned to carve the new figure of Burns' notorious witch.

49. *(Below) Arthur Levison beside the figurehead of* Loch Trool 1367/84 *which he carved to replace the one lost in collision in 1910. (Courtesy Sea Breezes)*

James Lindsay, Sunderland (51). James Lindsay made entries in the Trades Directories between 1819 and 1827, and in the records of James Laing his name appears against 11 ships between 1819 and 1823. *York 101/19* was the most extravagantly decorated at £33.4.0, while *Nereus 203/20*, *Cecrops 325/20* and *Plutus* of 1823 cost only £ 3.3.0 apiece. There followed a short break until James Lindsay carved for *Mary Laing 319/34* and *Derwent 368/35* at £22.0.0. In about 1852 another James Lindsay, son of John Lindsay took over and in 1852 began providing carved work for the Laing yard and he now had to share the work with others. *Merchantman 1018/52* earned Lindsay £30.0.0 and Nehemiah Williams of London, who carved the figurehead, received £15.0.0. *Antipodes 648/53* was shared with James Brooker of Maryport who provided the general carved work for £8.9.0 against Lindsay's £25.12.8. George Tate was the other carver on *Dunphaile Castle 7720/61* with Lindsay receiving £41.3.0 and Tate £13.10.0. In all between 1852 and 1880 he supplied figureheads, carved work and gilding for 88 ships from the James Laing yard. All the time he was working alongside other firms. In 1864 he was paid £96.11 for his efforts on *Uitenhage* while Elder received only £16.4.2. Melvin and Lindsay both supplied carved work for the steamer

Waldridge 662/68, receiving £9.0.0 and £1.15.0 respectively. When the steamer *General Havelock 472/61* was built she was extensively decorated with Robert Smith receiving the lion's share of the cost at £60.17.0 against Lindsay's £14.0.0. James Lindsay was also kept busy with orders from the Doxford shipyard between 1860 and 1876 working on about 55 of their vessels. Some of the entries in the Doxford books are detailed and it would appear that a lot of his work was 'architectural', but nevertheless profitable. For *Bengalese 1474/71* he cut carved work for £20.0.0 and brackets for £30.16.0. For *Stanton 817/70*, gilded trusses for £13.10.0, and *Victoria 2909/75* was carved and gilded for £173.10.3.

The ledgers which have survived from the Short Bros. yard show that James Lindsay worked for them on and off between 1872 and 1881. Among the ships for which he carved were *Shakespeare 1814/76*, £20.0.0, and *Regina 2376/81* which he shared with Hutton, receiving £24.6.0 against Hutton's £3.12.6.

John Lindsay, Sunderland.   In business at the same time was John Lindsay. In 1834 and 1835 the Doxford records contain two entries for small jobs worth a mere 10/6 and £1.11.1. The books of James Laing show that they placed orders with John Lindsay between 1847 and 1850 for seven of their ships. On five the work was shared with James Brooker of Maryport. For *Anglia 570/49* and *Talavera 916/50* Brooker carved the figureheads. For *Anglia* Brooker received £6.15.6 and Lindsay £14.1.0. For *Talavera* Lindsay's earnings were £22.15.0 and Brooker's £11.0.8. It did not always pay to be given the contract for carving the figurehead. It is highly likely that Brooker carved the figureheads for the other three: *Australasia 500/47*, *Camperdown 993/47* and *Minden 742/48*. In 1851 John Lindsay was employing in his workshop 6 men and 3 boys. The book about shipbuilding in Sunderland called "Where Ships are Born" states that all Pile's work was carved by John Lindsay (50) who was proud of his title, "carver and gilder by appointment to H.M.Queen Victoria." John Lindsay had been commanded to provide carved work for Windsor Castle. A newspaper report informs us that the figurehead of *Chowringhee 893/51*, built by William Pile portrayed a Bengalese native struggling with a tiger and it had been carved by John Lindsay.

T. Logan & Co., Glasgow.   This company cut some carved work for Stephen of Linthouse, stern carvings for the steam yacht *Mingary* built in 1925 for £8.7.6. with interior carved work for £4.0.0. When Stephens built three cargo liners for Elder & Fyffes they were asked to provide extensive internal decorative carvings: *Tortuguero 5285/21* £18.14.9, *Cavina 6907/24* £70.2.6, and *Ariguana 6746/26*, £118.6.0. Thomas Logan's name was first entered in the directories in 1910.

Logan & Venn, Liverpool.   There is no information available about any work which Logan & Venn may have done for Liverpool shipbuilders, but in a newspaper published in Ayr in 1839 we find a glowing description of the figurehead carved by Logan & Venn for the ship *Eglinton 99/39*, launched from the yard of Cowan & Sloans, Ayr. "Her appearance is very attractive, the figurehead being a representation of the Lord of the Tournament on horseback, at full tilt, beautifully carved in wood and gilded, while on the stern is a carved and gilded representation of the Arms of the Eglinton family, and the panelling is decorated with figures of horses at full speed. The end of the tiller is also carved in the shape of a horse's head." In records in Lancaster there are descriptions of the launching of small schooners from the yard of M. Simpson and to figureheads supplied by J. & J. Venn of Liverpool. For *Gauntlet 122/57* they carved a 3' 6" warrior holding a gauntlet glove for a cost of £4.10.0. For *Express 120/60* and *Kate 119/61* they cut:

	Express	*Kate*
3' 6" female figurehead	£3.10.0	£3.10.0
Carving stern ornament	1.10.0	1.12.6
Carving two trail boards	18/0	18/0
Carving two name boards	1. 1.0	1. 2.0

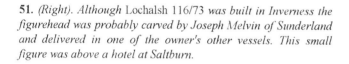

51. *(Above). This sketch is one of a number bearing the inscription "A. H. Messenger" which were drawn in about 1900 in the London docks. Onyx 427/64 was built by James Laing and the figurehead was carved by James Lindsay.*

51. *(Right). Although Lochalsh 116/73 was built in Inverness the figurehead was probably carved by Joseph Melvin of Sunderland and delivered in one of the owner's other vessels. This small figure was above a hotel at Saltburn.*

Hugh Logan and John and James Venn appear to have worked together until about 1843 when separate entries were put in Gore's Directory. Logan's name vanishes shortly after but John and James Venn continued in business until at least 1857.

Robert C. Lyness, Glasgow. The name of R. C. Lyness appears in two sets of shipyard records. In 1881 he cut figureheads and trail boards, as well as the general carved work for 8 ships from the Russell yard in Port Glasgow. He seems to have had a standard charge of £4.10.0 for a figurehead and £1.10.0 for the trail boards. As with most Russell sailing ships there was little money wasted on decoration and it varied from £2.2.0 for *Java 913/81* to £6.17.0 for *Rotomahana 1658/81*. He cut a billet head for *Bandeeth 724/82* which still cost £4.10.0, the last job he was to do for Russell. Another carver, Buchan, cut the interior work.

For two years Lyness received orders from William Denny, across the river from Greenock for fairly lucrative contracts which totalled £72.18.0 in 1880 and £304.10.3 in 1881. The 1871 census shows that the family were all carvers and gilders. Robert Lyness, the father aged 51, Robert C.Lyness then aged 24, and the nephew Joseph McCreally aged 18.

Thomas McCracken, Glasgow. Thomas McCracken came on the scene late in the 19th. Century and his name has only cropped up in the cost books of Scotts of Greenock. He carved for seven of their ships, among them the well-known *Hougomont 2428/97* (53) and *Archibald Russell 2385/05*. He charged £4.10.0 for the *Hougomont* and £8.0.0 for *Archibald Russell*. The timber for the latter figurehead cost £6.14.4. His last job for Scotts was the billethead and carved work for *Carnarvon 514/06*, a lighthouse tender built on the lines of a steam yacht. McCracken charged £8.10.0 for the billethead and £7.19.0 for the timber. He also worked on the steam yacht *Margarita 1792/00*, sharing the £113.9.11 bill with four other carvers.

Robert McGowan, (sometimes McGown), of Greenock and Glasgow. McGowan carved for J. &.G. Thomson of Clydebank between 1854 and 1865. Only a few of the cashbook entries give the name of the vessel but they included some of the Clyde paddle steamers. Although

Iona 174/55 had no figurehead she was extensively decorated internally and cost £13.15.6. for carving. His best order was for *Thessalia 1169/55* which brought him in £30.14.0. His payments from this yard peaked in 1855 at £132.9.0 but by 1865 preference was being given to other carvers and he received his last payments totalling only £6.6.0 for the year.

Some daybooks from Scott & Sons of Bowling have been preserved and at least from 1862 to 1865 McGowan seems to have enjoyed the complete confidence of the Bowling yard. Only two vessels were named. *Caroline* of 1862 required for her carved work 9 cu. ft. of yellow pine @ 3/11 per cu.ft. and of other timbers 8½ cu. ft. @ 2/10 and 1½ cu. ft. @ 3½d. McGowan carved three small figureheads in the same year for between £2.0.0 and £2.10.0, one of them for *Chase*. A larger one in 1865 cost £4.10.0. Carving the trailboards cost £1.10.0 and the decoration of the stern £3.0.0. He also received some orders from Scott's of Greenock but only cash entries have been found totalling £42.2.0 in 1863 and £26.5.0 in 1865.

He was born in 1823 and lived in Greenock from 1847 to 1855, calling himself "a ship and ornamental carver". After moving to Glasgow he called himself "a carver in wood". He died in 1869.

Andrew McKay, Aberdeen.   Andrew McKay was the first carver to execute work for Alexander Hall in Aberdeen, though his early orders were pretty basic. After cutting outside carving and the stern decorations for *Barbara 164/17* for £5.0.0 he was asked to carve and gild several hawse pipe surrounds. There was a gap until 1835 when he was instructed to carve a couple of figureheads, *Jardine 58/35*, a male bust for £2.0.0, and *Earl of Fife 82/36*, another male bust for £4.1.6. In the Hall books there is a single entry for a figurehead carved by James McKay, a female bust for *Europa 124/34*.

Neil McLean, Glasgow.   Thomson & Spiers opened shipyards in Greenock and Troon in 1840, only to close down in 1844. Neil McLean carved a figurehead for a barque *Janet Wilson*

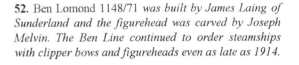

52. *Otago 1048/69 was built by Robert Duncan of Port Glasgow during the short period when McMillan & Bathgate were their contract carvers. The cost book names Bathgate as the carver. (Courtesy Alexander Turnbull Library, Wellington, New Zealand)*

52. *Ben Lomond 1148/71 was built by James Laing of Sunderland and the figurehead was carved by Joseph Melvin. The Ben Line continued to order steamships with clipper bows and figureheads even as late as 1914.*

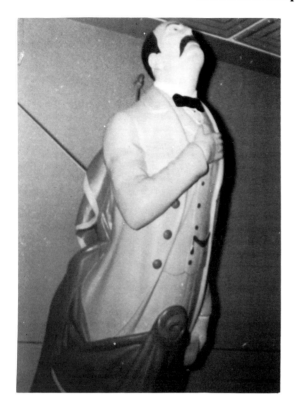

53. *This is the figurehead of* W. T. Lewis. *Built as* Robert Duncan 2166/91 *he had to be 'shaved' by his new American owners. In common with most owner type heads he holds a scroll in his hand. The carver was John Roberts.*

53. Hougomont 2428/97 *was a well known ship built by Scott's of Greenock. The figurehead was carved by Thomas McCracken and is preserved in the museum at Mariehamn.*

McMillan & Bathgate, Greenock.   George Bathgate and Hamilton McMillan went into partnership in 1866 as McMillan & Bathgate. By 1871 they had expanded their business and were employing 10 men and 10 boys. In 1879 McMillan retired and left the whole of the business to Bathgate, though the title remained unchanged. Falling orders led to a reduction in the work force to 4 men, 5 boys and one girl by 1881, and finally to bankruptcy which was finalised in 1888.

Robert Duncan of Port Glasgow sent orders during the period 1867 to 1882, during which time they completed 30 figureheads. In the Duncan cost books George Bathgate receives the credit of carving 25 of them. Among the figureheads which he carved was that of *Otago 349/69*, now preserved in New Zealand (52). The total cost of the carved work was only £20.0.0. The most expensive contract which he fulfilled was *Rozelle 1286/68* which brought in £59.2.10.

Another good customer was Scott's of Greenock for whom McMillan & Bathgate provided carved work for at least 41 ships between 1868 and 1884. They frequently had to share the carved work with other companies, usually James Allan, junior, or M. & J. Allan. Sometimes the Allans got the lion's share. On *Jessie Readman 962/69* M. & J. Allan received £54.19.6, while McMillan & Bathgate got only 9/3. At other times the work was more evenly divided, as with *Priam 2039/70* where, for the outside carved work the Allans were paid £15.0.0, the others receiving £50.18.9 for the interior carvings. McMillan & Bathgate were rather guilty of not having work ready on time and Scotts had to keep pressing them for delivery. When the firm went bankrupt the legal papers listed the names of those who owed them money and among them were several shipbuilders including A. Shearer, J. Russell and A. & J. Inglis of Pointhouse, Glasgow. John E. Scott were shipbuilders in Greenock from 1874 until 1879. McMillan & Bathgate cut carved work for *Ocean King 2449/78*, *Devon 1856/78* and *Fire Queen 474/79*, all steamships. When Scott's closed they owed £65.9.0 for this work. Bathgate's father had been a carver and gilder in a partnership called Bathgate & Wilson, but there is no evidence that they carried out ship work.

Peter McMillan, Aberdeen.   Peter McMillan had a short spell on the books of Alexander

Hall from 1848 to 1850 starting with a "reindeer" for *Reindeer 328/48* at £8.2.9. His female figurehead for *Princeza 149/49* cost £11.8.3. In all he carved for six of Hall's ships.

Archibald McVicar, Greenock.   McVicar was in the Directories from 1821 until his death in 1861. The only reference found was a small job for John O. Scott of Greenock in 1861.

Marshall, Sunderland.   The Laing Shipyard paid a carver named Marshall £4.5.0 for the carved work for the schooner *James Cooke 204/36.*

James Martin, Whitehaven.   In the Trades Directory for 1869 James Martin called himself a "carver and gilder" but by 1883 he was a "carver and gilder, (Ship)". However, in 1886, shortly after he had moved to new premises, his bill-head describes him as a "carver, gilder, and frame manufacturer". An unusual comment at the bottom of his bill-head reads: "In possession of all ornamental frame moulds formerly used by the late Mr. John Askew." James Martin held two shares in the Whitehaven Shipbuilding Co. Ltd. which presumably gave him an advantage when quoting for carved work for their vessels.

Meiklejohn & Young, Glasgow.   None of the records which have survived from Clyde shipyards contain the name of this company who described themselves as "ship carvers" in the 1859 directory. In the 1871 census George Meiklejohn described himself as "carver and gilder" while Samuel Young called himself a "master carver". At this time they employed 2 men and 4 boys.

Joseph Melvin, Sunderland.   Joseph Melvin "ship carver and gilder" was kept working hard for the yard of James Laing of Sunderland from 1868 to 1887 during which time he produced work for 4 sailing ships and 120 steamers (51). From the start he was sharing the contracts with W.L.Snaith or less frequently with James Lindsay until about 1875 after which he had the field to himself on the ships on which he was employed. Although he was primarily occupied in providing figureheads and carved work for steamships, many were profusely decorated. Most of them brought him in less than £20.0.0 but some were worth more to him. *Durban 2878/77* was priced at £230.0.2, while *Mexican 4668/82* cost £204.0.0. These were exceptions. More typical was £59.3.5 for *Ben Venue 1515/70* and £33.9.6 for *Campeador 1258/84,* a clipper bowed liner. The composite clipper *Torrens 1335/75* was very ornate with a bill for her carved work of £170.10.6 which included a figurehead which was the likeness of the young lady who launched her, the daughter of Captain H. R. Angel. Melvin shared the work on *Columba 1031/72* and *Estabana de Antunano 1804/84* with the Hellyer family.

Other shipbuilders employed Melvin. There is a single entry in the Bartram books for £9.10.0 for carved work but no ship is named. For Short Bros. he cut carved work for 4 steamers including *Cherubini 1776/80* for £49.8.6. and *James Westoll 1990/84* for £26.14.6. A less likely customer was the shipbuilder Robert Stewart of Inverness who went out of business in 1879 owing Melvin £13.7.6. There were no ship carvers in the area and as Stewart was a ship owner as well it was just as handy for him to have his figureheads carved in Sunderland. He built *Lochalsh 116/73* (51) in 1873 and her figurehead which stood in Saltburn would have been carved by Melvin.

Thomas Millar, Glasgow.   Thomas Millar, carver and gilder, carried out carved work in 1868 for William Donald, shipbuilder of Paisley at a cost of £4.10.0. His name only appears in the directories between 1868 and 1871.

John Valentine Moloney, Hull.   The trades directories carry the name of John Valentine Moloney, "ship and ornamental carver" from at least 1848 to 1869. Nothing is known about him.

Murray & Duguid, Aberdeen.   The cost books of Alexander Hall contain but a single

55. *For £6.1.0. A. & D. G. Reid provided the external carving for* Balclutha 1716/86. *With no trailboards there can have been very little other decorative carving. The figurehead has had to be replaced with a new one carved by Greg Powlesland.*

entry for this partnership. For *Rosalind 365/85* they cut trailboards for £1.10.0.

William Nielson, Paisley.   William Nielson, carver and gilder, worked in Paisley between 1857 and 1882. In 1881 he received £15.2.0 from the shipbuilding yard of Campbell & Co., John Millar and Peter Semple of Paisley for work which he had carried out for them.

Henry Nutter, Whitehaven.   The Nutter family of Whitehaven worked as ship carvers in the latter years of the 18th. century. When *Scipio 180/1790* was launched from the yard of James Shepherd, Henry Nutter, (now in his 60s), carved the figurehead, which was "allowed to be a piece of excellent workmanship." His son Ellis worked with him as a carver and also painted the figures as they were completed. Ellis Nutter died in 1809.

Tom Owen, Appledore.   In his book Merchant Schooners Basil Greenhill tells us that Tom Owen of Appledore was the craftsman generally employed to carve bow decorations for vessels built beside the River Torridge.

George Pate, Sunderland.   James Laing of Sunderland gave George Pate orders for major carved work on ten of their vessels between 1839 and 1843. His charges varied from £3.0.0 for *Charles Kerr* of 1842 to £16.0.0 for *Crecy 720/43*. There followed a break of seven years and in 1850 he was asked for stern carvings for *Osbert 315/51* for £4.12.0 and stern galleries for another vessel, un-named, at £10.0.6. He shared the carved work on *Wreath 295/50* with James Brooker of Maryport.

Albert Pearn, Polruan.   In his research notes the late C. H. Ward-Jackson makes reference to Albert Pearn who worked around 1897 as a figurehead carver, restorer and painter in the ship-building yard of J. Slade and Sons, Polruan, near Fowey in Cornwall.

Quinn & McKenzie, Dundee.   This partnership first appears in the directories in 1882. In 1884 Peter Quinn is described as a "ship carver" while Robert McKenzie calls himself a "wood carver". In 1885 only Peter Quinn's name is recorded, now as "wood carver".

A. & D. G. Reid, Glasgow.   In the 1861 census records Alexander Reid is defined as a "wood carver". In the 1871 census he is called "a foreman wood carver aged 37, with an apprentice carver aged 15", his son Douglas.

He and his son set up business on their own as A. & D. G. Reid. The date of this move is not known but the first time that the name appears is in the records of Charles Connell is 1882. Connell's gave them orders from 1882 right up to 1898, though at an average of £16 per vessel the contracts were not exactly profitable. The ships that were built by Connell cannot have had much decorative work on them. Their *Vimiera 2164/91* netted the Reids £16.19.4, compared with the earlier *Vimiera* launched in Sunderland in 1851 for which W. H. Bridges received £27.10.0. Correspondence from Connell's to the Reids has been kept and covers the period 1883 to 1898. When the yard sent the block for No.141, *Charles Connell 1724/85*, they "hoped that Reid's would give us a good job as we have given you preference. The figure is to be a demi female and is to be reconciled when in position. The price is £5.0.0." As work on *Earl of Aberdeen 2205/86*, No.145 proceeded, a photograph of that gentleman was delivered to Reid's with instructions that "the figure is to be represented with an earl's coronet and robe, and is to be finished off with trailboards 8 to 9 feet long. Please take good care of the photograph and return it."

For No.151, *Helicon 1663/87* the owner wished a female figure and sent a sketch of Euterpe the muse of wind instruments. The figure was to be used as a guide but the flutes had to be left off. Then followed the vague instruction that "the figure has to have a good form and a nice face." The shipyard was continually having to chase the carvers for their carved work: "Please let us know when we may send for the figure for No.179 (*Este 1420/91*)." Shortly afterwards: "Please let us know at the earliest when we may send for the figure for No. 183 (*R. P. Rithet 1080/92*)." By No. 187 (*Saint Mungo 1955/92*) Connell's were getting exasperated, saying, "Can you not possibly give us the figure for No. 187. Unless you cannot do better for delivery we shall have to divide our orders." Even that threat had little effect: "We would like the figure for No.191 (*Marion Josiah 2394/92*) by Wednesday at the latest. Friday will be too late for us." Anyone who believes that the figureheads on the models of ships are an accurate representation will be disappointed to learn that Connell's ordered from Reid six model figureheads at a time, one male, five female.

The Reids provided the carved work for *Balclutha 1689/86* at a cost of £16.2.0 (54). When the carver Greg Powlesland was asked to carve a new figurehead for *Balclutha* in 1975 he had to strip forty-five layers of paint from the existing carving to get down to the original wood. He was impressed by the workmanship of the old carver and commented on the confident way in which a large chisel had been used to cut the dress and the body, contrasting it with the delicacy with which the hands and head had been shaped.

By the end of the century the Reids were among the few carvers left in Scotland and lesser shipyards from other areas came to them for carved work. The Reids seem to have been unlucky with their small business contacts. Grangemouth Dockyard failed in 1893 owing them £64.0.3, probably for two sailing ships which the Dockyard had just completed, one of which was *Cara 1513/92*. H. McIntyre of Alloa, who gave up in 1895, were £48.19.11 in debt, a considerable sum at the end of the century for carved work. Other customers were John Scott & Co. of Kinghorn in Fife who went out of business in 1901 owing the Reids £7.0.0., and Cumming & Ellis of Inverkeithing who had an outstanding debt of £3.7.0 when they started their bankruptcy proceedings in 1899.

John Roberts, Port Glasgow (17) .   Roberts' name has not been found in any directory, but he appears on the Clyde scene in 1880 when he shared the carved work on Robert Duncan's *Sea Queen 385/80*, a steam yacht, costing in all £15.8.0. Three other contracts followed for sundry carved work on small steamers. It was 1890 before Duncan's awarded him carving work again, this time on a series of full-rigged sailing ships. Their requirements were for plain figureheads with few fancy extras which cost between £5.9.6 and £10.10.0 per vessel. His last job for them was 4/- for a carving for a steamer. In all he worked on 20 vessels from the Duncan yard including *Howard D. Troop 2165/92* and *John Ena 2842/92*. In 1882 he received his first order from Russell's of Port Glasgow for trailboards for a barque for which he was paid 16/-. From then on Roberts carved for all the Russell ships providing them with figureheads and trailboards for about £6.15.0. and general carved work for £4.0.0 to £9.0.0. He cut the name for the shallow draught paddle steamer *Annie Laurie 20/83* on her paddle boxes for 18/6 and a rope moulding for the stern of the paddle steamer *Lady Margaret 144/83* for £1.8.0. Some of the cost book entries give details of the work involved. No.156-*Rhine 1556/86* to John Roberts, 30th. Nov. 1886.

To carving and gilding 63 ft. of neck moulding   @ 8½d   £2. 4.0

---do---	66 trusses @ 4/3	3. 8.0	
---do---	3 teak trusses @ 2/4	7/0	
---do---	demi-figure and trail boards	5.10.0	
Reducing head of figure to clear bowsprit		4/0	
One truss		4/3	Total £11.18.4.

No.244-*Port Stanley 2187/90* to John Roberts, 31st.Oct.1890 (6).

Cutting head for model		5/6	
Carving and gilding neck moulding	80 ft. @ 8½d	2.16.8	
---do---	18 trusses @ 4/3	3.16.6	
Mirror frame 54" x 36" =15' 6	@ 7/2	1.13.7	
Pediment		12/0	
4 teak trusses	@ 2/6	10/0	
Demi-figure and trailboards from stock		3.10.0	
Gilder to touch up saloon		10/6	Total £13.9.9.

Roberts had a standard charge of £5.10.0 for a figurehead and even a billethead cost the same, and when he was not busy he would carve a standard female figurehead and keep it in stock, selling it for £3.15.0. Should the customer require that the figure should represent a specific person a charge of £2.15.0 was made to cover the cost of the alteration. For most vessels he also carved a figurehead for the builders' model. One of his most expensive figureheads was the one which he cut for *Marie Rickmers 3813/90* for which he was paid £14.15.0, which included the trailboards. From around 1890 many of the cost book entries show that he was working from a photograph as he carved the figurehead. There are some unusual entries. When the figurehead of *Professor Koch 1476/91* was finished a pair of copper spectacles was purchased to complete it, at a cost of 5/-. The figurehead of *Brilliant 3609/01* needed 12 brilliants @ 12/6 to set it off properly. In 1891 Roberts carved a likeness of Robert Duncan for a four masted barque of that name *2160/91*, complete with a figurehead sporting a typical Victorian beard. In 1910 the vessel was sold to owners in San Francisco and renamed *William T. Lewis*, but as Mr. Lewis did not have a beard the figurehead had to be 'shaved' to suit (53). Although *Brilliant* was the last vessel from the Russell yard to have a figurehead Roberts continued to do other carved work for them right up to 1920.

When he first began to work in Port Glasgow John Roberts received orders in 1880-1882 from Scotts' of Greenock for general carved work for six steamships. He had to share the work with Joseph Humphreys and generally he got the 'smaller slice of the cake'. *Dragut 556/80* and *La Valette 553/80* brought Roberts £6.10.0 while Humphreys received £78.3.3.

There is preserved in Australia the figurehead of *Glenpark 1959/97* built by A. Rodger & Co. of Port Glasgow and descendants of John Roberts have evidence that it was he who carved this figurehead(17). He apparently made a good living out of the carving business, being able to employ a servant. His sons worked with him until he died, after plying his trade for nearly 60 years.

Adam Robertson, Newcastle. In the 1837 Trades Directory there appears an entry for Adam Robertson, "House and ship carver and picture frame maker."

Archibald Robertson, Greenock and Liverpool.(59). Archibald Robertson was the earliest known figurehead carver in Greenock but we have only one record of the work which he carried out while there. There lived in the town of Kilbarchan a local 'worthy' named Habbie Simpson, a piper, and in about 1821 Robertson was asked to carve a statue of him which was erected in a niche on a church steeple. Although the old wooden carving has long since gone a bronze replica stands in its place. Robertson carved a figurehead of James Watt, probably for the steamer *James Watt 142/24,* built in Liverpool, and he was guided by a sculptor called Chantry who was engaged in making a bronze bust of the famous inventor at that time. Although he moved to Liverpool prior to 1825 he must have made quite a reputation for himself as a figurehead carver, as some shipbuilders on the Clyde still went to him for figures for their ships. In 1833 Denny of

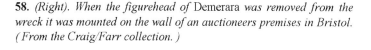

58. *(Above). Euterpe was one of the Muses and her image was mounted on the bows of* Euterpe *1197/63 launched by Gibson & Co., Ramsay, Isle of Man. This figurehead was the work of George Sutherland.*

58. *(Right). When the figurehead of* Demerara *was removed from the wreck it was mounted on the wall of an auctioneers premises in Bristol. (From the Craig/Farr collection.)*

Dumbarton paid him £49.3.5 for "figureheads and carvings" and again in 1834 £7.14.6 for a "figurehead". Further orders followed:

1847-to Archibald Robertson, carving for *Northman 185/47* .Yd. 9

Carving demi figure	£6. 6.0.
Timber for arms	4/8
--do-- for face	2/9
--do-- for spear and battleaxe	2/4
Materials and packing	5/0
Carving quarter badges	4. 4.0
--do-- stern	5.10.0
5 drops	1. 0.0
Medallion, freight and packing	17/6

Even as late as 1852 when the Clyde had reputable carvers of its own Denny was still sending orders to Liverpool calling for two shield heads for *Balbec 838/52* at £90.0.0, which was a considerable sum at that time.

Another customer was the Scotts yard at Greenock who paid a bill in 1825 for £1.17.7 and later wrote to Robertson in 1827 for a figurehead of a Harlequin, (*Frolic 100/27*) having seen his figurehead on the brig *Tickler* in 1826 with which they had been very impressed. It took 3 months for him to complete and deliver the Harlequin and Scotts were threatening to cancel the order and go elsewhere. They wrote once more in 1828 with a request for a figure "appropriate to Arethusa" (*Arethusa 322/28*) and in 1829 for a bust of John Scott for a vessel of that name: "a striding or stepping off figure whichever is most used at present." They placed further orders in 1833 and 1849. In 1833 they had on the stocks *Kirkman Finlay 430/34* and for her they required a bust rather than a full length figure. Also they requested that "it should have drapery thrown over the shoulder rather than modern dress which looks stiff." Delivery was requested for July. In September they were advised that Robertson was working from a sketch which he had made of Mr. Finlay, but no delivery date was forthcoming. In October they were getting desperate and asked for the figure no later than the end of the month. In the middle of November there was till no sign of the bust and Scott's advised Robertson that they wanted it delivered on a ship sailing at the end of the month. as no further letters were recorded we must assume that at last the bust of Mr. Finlay was delivered, albeit four months late. In 1849 they were asking for another figurehead, despite Robertson's bad delivery on the previous occasion. This time it was for a ship for the East India trade (*Seringapatam 587/49*) and they were more explicit about the figurehead. They thought that "it should be about seven feet high, exclusive of the scroll, a male figure in eastern costume, one hand resting on a sword or scimitar and pointing with the other. It would not look well for the hands to be loaded with anything." Then followed the strange, and contradictory comment that "If you think that an eastern female figure would be more showy and look better, do it in that style." There is no record of which style Robertson carved. The shipyard only gave him a month in which to complete the carving for which they paid him £13.10.11, but they thought that "the figure had a good appearance." Even as late as 1865 there

59. *This sketch taken from the builder's drawing shows the imposing figure which Robertson was to carve for* Europa 1834/48.

was a payment of £6.6.0 for unspecified work. One letter, undated, but probably 1863, appears to relate to a vessel which was to be renamed *Albion 668/63* and which apparently already had a figurehead fitted but the owners wished to change the figurehead as well as the name. The letter ended on a cynical note. "Removing the figurehead will cause a considerable amount of delay as the bolts and bowsprit fastening will all have to come out to get at the bolts holding the figurehead and we shall have to keep the deck of the forecastle up until a new one can be got in. The carvers here are all overwhelmed with work and there might be a delay there also. The head actually on is sufficiently masculine to personify the mythical personage which would perhaps be better portrayed by a figure of a chalk cliff than by either a man or woman."

He is understood to have provided figureheads for several early Cunard steamers built in Clyde yards. From the yard of Robert Steele of Greenock, *America 1826/48*, *Niagara 1825/48*, *Africa 2226/50* and *Asia /2227/50*, and from James Wood of Port Glasgow, *Europa 1834/48*. In 1854 Barr & Shearer who built ships in Ardrossan had Robertson carve for them "An excellent likeness of the Emperor Napoleon III for the vessel of that name." (*Napoleon III 862/55*) (64).

After Archibald Robertson settled down in Liverpool he produced figureheads and carved work for the Laird shipyard, among them *Vulcan 1400 b.m./45*, renamed *Birkenhead* before her launch for service as a troop ship, "a figure of Vulcan holding a hammer in one hand and the bolts of Jove in the other." In 1843 he described himself as a "Ship carver, block and pump maker". Later he was joined by Robert Robertson and the name of the firm became A. & R. Robertson. The date would be about 1854 as an account for J. & G. Thomson of Clydebank for carved work for their *Jura 2240/54* for £54.8.3. was paid to A. & R. Robertson. The new partnership carried out work for Laird's, Royden's, and other shipyards building for the Cunard and Allan Lines. In 1860 the entry in the Trades Directory read, "Block and mast makers, and ship carvers". James Brooker of Maryport served his apprenticeship with Robertson starting in 1828.

Rudd of Barnstaple.   In an article "Arts and Crafts of an Old Seaport" in the Transactions of the Devonshire Association, Bideford, 1948, we read:

"Around 1900 the figureheads for Cock's new schooners *Rosie 95/85*, *Maud 120/96* and *Katie 124/03* were carved by a dear old man who came over here from Barnstaple, a Mr. Rudd."

J. Rutherford & Sons, Aberdeen.   J. Rutherford & Sons received two orders from Alexander Hall for minor carved work. *Port Jackson 2212/82* earned them £6.12.0 and they shared

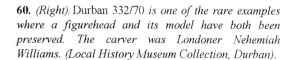

60. *(Above). This is the sketch which Nehemiah Williams prepared for* Gold Digger 152/54.

60. *(Right).* Durban 332/70 *is one of the rare examples where a figurehead and its model have both been preserved. The carver was Londoner Nehemiah Williams. (Local History Museum Collection, Durban).*

the work with three other carving firms, the figurehead being carved by M. & J. Allan of Glasgow. In the same year they decorated the steamer *Glentilt 477/82* for £1.11.6, the only money spent on decorative work.

William Rutledge, Sunderland.   The name of William Rutledge is recorded against 12 vessels built by William Doxford & Sons of Sunderland over a period 1860 to 1866. Many of the contracts were shared with James Lindsay. Rutledge's efforts are described only as "carved work" but he was receiving annual payments which rose from £8.6.0 in 1860 to £109.4.0 in 1865.

Robert Saddler Scott, Newcastle.   Robert Saddler Scott came from a family of carvers and gilders going back to the early 1800s. In 1802 his father had been apprenticed to Richard Farrington to learn the trade of joiner, ship carver and gilder for a period of seven years. R. S. Scott put an entry in the Trades Directory in 1869 describing himself as a "house and ship carver". A sample of his work was still extant in 1966 in the form of a huge wooden mask representing the River Tyne, portraying a head with a beard in three plaits surmounted by a basket containing coals and surrounded by various emblems of the trades on the Tyne.

William Shanks, Glasgow.   William Shanks worked as a foreman for Thomas Kay in Dumbarton and when Kay died in 1852 his widow took on Shanks as a partner and the firm became Kay & Shanks. In 1857 he left and set up on his own as a figurehead carver in Glasgow. He took with him some of the 'good will' of Denny of Dumbarton who gave him orders over the next six years, providing carved work for extravagantly decorated steamships. The *Ostrich 624/59* cost *£213.9.8, Heron 624/59* came to £214.19.8 and *Norwegian 2449/61* brought in £292.12.3. There was an unusual entry in the Denny ledgers, a payment of £412.13.11 for carved work for stock, paid in 1862, which must have kept William Shanks busy for quite a while. This, however, was the last payment he received from Denny.

Jonathan Shepherd, Whitehaven.   Thos. & Jno. Brocklebank, the well known ship owners were also shipbuilders with a yard in Whitehaven from whence they launched about 117 ships of all sizes between 1801 and 1865. For most of this period their carved work was supplied by

John Askew, but in 1861 the yard turned to Jonathan Shepherd for their ship decoration, an arrangement which continued until 1865 when the last ship was launched. During this period 7 vessels were built, all large enough to have had figureheads. Only a few of the ledger entries bore the ship's name:

30th.Nov.1862. *Ariel 130/62*. Carved work, head and stern	£5. 5.0
30th.Nov.1863. *Everest 571/63*. Carving head, stern and trailboards	16.10.0
30th.June 1865. *Mahanada 1003/65*. Head, stern, and trailboards	17. 0.0
Name boards	3.10.0

This was the last vessel to be launched from the Brocklebank yard in Whitehaven, and she was lost as *Sigrid* in 1904.

Shepherd's prices were not very cheap as he charged £3.10.0 for name boards, a price for which other carvers would have cut a figurehead. He seems to have been an odd choice as a replacement for John Askew, an acknowledged expert ship carver, as, at no time did he describe himself as a "ship carver". The entries in the Trades Directories indicate a variety of skills from 1855, "cabinet maker, and joiner" to 1873, "Cabinet maker, upholsterer and carver and gilder."

John Smith, Aberdeen. The Hall cost books contain one entry under the name of John Smith who carved a female figurehead for their *Gazelle 121/40* at a cost of £6.0.0.

Robert Smith, Sunderland. Robert Smith called himself "a turner and carver". He obtained orders from the James Laing shipyard between 1865 and 1871, though during that time he worked on only ten ships. Despite the fact that they were all steamships the amount of money spent on them was quite astonishing. For his share of the work on *C. J. Textor 673/69* he received £100.4.6. The other carvers Snaith and Lindsay got £9.9.0 and £13.10.0 respectively. Another money spinner was *Good Hope 1221/68* at £67.0.6, other work on the ship being done by Lindsay and Snaith once more. In the 1876 directory Smith was calling himself a "painter".

W.L.Snaith, Sunderland. Snaith described himself as a "carver, gilder and fret cutter". Although he provided carved work for the Laing yard, for no less than 36 steamships and 4 sailing ships, he played only a minor part with work valued from 14/- on *Abana 727/71* to £15.12.0 on the composite ship *Collingrove 861/69*. He worked beside better known carvers such as Kyle, Melvin and Lindsay. In 1896 he was given two orders each worth £2.8.0 for the carved work for two steamers.

George Sutherland, Dumbarton and Glasgow. George Sutherland was born in Leith in 1829, son of the ship carver Alexander Sutherland. While George was still a schoolboy the family moved to Glasgow where he learned his trade. In 1853, hoping to better himself he emigrated to America but in 1856 he was back in Scotland, in Dumbarton, where he advertised that he was setting up his own business (62). In 1861 he moved once more, this time to Glasgow. He was fortunate in that he received a number of valuable orders from the Denny yard, among them *Columbia 392/60* for which he was paid £72.11.6, and *Hungarian 2449/61* which netted him £49.0.0 for a scrollhead and £91.14.6 for general carved work. When *Hibernian 2449/61* was launched the local newspaper wrote: "The carved work, by Mr. George Sutherland of Glasgow, is deserving of the highest commendation. The figurehead, a more than half length figure of St. Patrick is well executed and forms a fine ornament to the bow of the vessel. Ireland's patron saint also makes his appearance in various places, and heads with thoroughly Irish faces are introduced in the carved work at all appropriate points." The last order which they gave him was for *Orissa 359/63* for which he was paid £64.3.0. The 1861 census shows that he was working on his own in Glasgow. When Gibson, McDonald & Arnold of Ramsey, Isle of Man, were building *Euterpe 1197/63* they engaged George Sutherland to carve as her figurehead the representation of the Greek goddess of that name (58).

In 1864 George Sutherland emigrated to Australia with his family.

MIRROR FRAMES! PICTURE FRAMES!! PIER TABLES!!!

GEORGE SUTHERLAND,
SHIP AND ORNAMENTAL CARVER AND GILDER,
ARTIZAN PLACE,
DUMBARTON,

BEGS to intimate to the Gentry and Inhabitants of Dumbarton and surrounding District, that he is now prepared to undertake work in all departments of the Business, and hopes from the superior style of workmanship, and a moderate rate of prices, to merit a share of their patronage.

Designs for MIRROR FRAMES, PICTURE FRAMES, and PIER TABLES furnished in the purest and most approved styles.

G. S. is satisfied that the Style of Work and Rates of Charges will bear comparison with any house in the trade.

GEORGE SUTHERLAND,
ARTIZAN PLACE, DUMBARTON.

George Tate, Sunderland.   George Tate began working for the James Laing shipyard in 1843 with a repair on the figurehead of *New Zealand 455/42* for £1.10.0. He carved a figurehead for *Abyssinia 669/44* in 1844 for £6.0.0 with decorative work for £17.6.0. He cut carved work for ten more vessels up to 1848 receiving payments ranging from £2.19.6 for *Garland 305/49* to £12.0.0 for *Bannockburn 757/45*. The last time that the word 'figurehead' appears against Tate's name is in 1859 when he was paid £8.0.0 for a head for *Sir J. Lawrence 698/59*, with £19.0.0 for decorative work. Until the last entry in 1861 the term 'carved work' is recorded against each item. The Doxford yard gave him contracts on several occasions for unnamed ships. In 1854 he executed a figurehead for £9.10.0 and in 1858 another for £8.14.0. In 1866 they awarded him three jobs totalling £40.0.0.

J. D. Thompson, Newcastle.   Two entries are recorded in the books of John Readhead & Sons of South Shields against the name of J. D. Thompson, carver, £42.1.0 in 1873 and £15.0.0 in 1874, each a total for the year. In his advertisement as a carver in the 1861 Ward's Directory he included the title "ship decorator".

J. D. THOMPSON,
CARVER & GILDER,
LOOKING GLASS & PICTURE FRAME
MANUFACTURER,
ORNAMENTAL, HOUSE, & SHIP DECORATOR,
48, HOWARD STREET, NORTH SHIELDS.

Henry White, London.   In 1820 bankruptcy proceedings were begun against James Warwick of Rotherhithe and on the list of creditors was Henry White of Rotherhithe, ship carver, asking for £29.0.0.

John Whitelaw, Greenock.   John Whitelaw was one of the late arrivals on the scene. Robert Duncan of Port Glasgow gave him orders for secondary carved work for most of their vessels between 1891 and 1907. In 1900 Scott's of Greenock brought him in to do inside carving for the steam yacht *Margarita* on which four other carvers were engaged, the total cost coming to £113.9.11 of which Whitelaw received £14.14.0. One other order was for the steam yacht *Suevuna 62/01* on which only 3/- was spent.

Nehemiah Williams, London.   Nothing has been found in official sources about Williams' work on merchant ships except that he carved a figurehead at a cost of £15.0.0 for *Merchantman 1018/52* built by Jas. Laing of Sunderland. However other items give us more information about this carver. In the Local History Museum in Durban is the figurehead from *Durban 332/70* (60) while, in the National Maritime Museum in London is a model of that figurehead. Even more important is the discovery of two albums of sketches by Nehemiah Williams. A great many of the sketches show a full length figure in the "stepping off" mode which was somewhat old fashioned by this time but these may have been intended for the Blackwall Frigates many of which were owned by Wigram whose name appears on at least 13 of the pages. As with the sketchbook of A. P. Elder most of the drawings bear no name though many give the name of a shipbuilder. What little information there is, is sufficient to let us see that Nehemiah Williams had clients (or prospective clients) over a wide area. Among the shipbuilders named are Asplet and Esneuf, both of Jersey, Harvey of Littlehampton, May & Thwaites and Bally, both of Shoreham. The name of J. Watson of Banff appears against a sketch of *Diana*. A number of vessels named were for London owners but built in yards other than those on the Thames. For *African 880/53*, built in Sunderland the sketch shows a negro holding a book, probably a Bible. *Harkaway 899/52* was built by Alex. Stephen in their Dundee yard but her figurehead was carved by James Hutton. *Onward 571/60* was built by Calman of Dundee. *Hanover 1045/53* was built in Shields by Marshall. Other countries which appear on the sketches are Norway, Sweden, and even Boston, U.S.A. *Doncaster 221/37*, although built before his time required extensive repairs in 1855 and 1858 which presumably included a new figurehead, a jockey with a whip in one hand and the reins in the other. *Gold Digger 152/54*, built in Sunderland and owned in London, shows a prospector with his pick in his hand and his pipe in his mouth (60).

Nehemiah Williams tried with limited success to obtain orders from the Admiralty. (See under Naval Carvers).

Robert Price Williams, Bristol. In 1815 Robert Price Williams established a business as a ship carver in Bristol. Around 1830 he took on as an apprentice his grandson John Robert Anderson and in 1835 he was joined by Robert and Thomas Williams who had been working in Rotherhithe in London. Robert senior died in 1847 and the firm became R. & T. Williams. The only figurehead found so far attributed to the Williams business is that of *Demerara* of 1851 (58). She was wrecked as she was being launched and the figurehead was erected in Bristol. In 1868 Robert Williams retired and John Anderson assumed control.

James Wishart, Aberdeen. James Wishart first appears in the books of Alexander Hall in 1851, when at the age of 24, he cut secondary carvings on *Dunrobin Castle 545/51* for £12.12.0, the figurehead being carved by Robert Hall of London. It was 1855 before Wishart carved his first figurehead for Hall, that of *Schomberg 2284/55* for £5.19.4½. The other carved work being carried out by George Hughes. Wishart and Hughes shared the work on nearly eighty ships launched from the Hall yard up until 1877, taking turns to carve the figureheads. From time to time another carver was brought in to cut the figurehead, Robert Hall and Hellyer of London or M. & J. Allan of Glasgow. The contracts from Hall did not bring in much money as 52 of them did not exceed £10.0.0 and the clipper ship *Ocean Mail 630/60* brought him in only 11/-. His best order was for *Bay of Naples 1615/75*, an iron ship, for which he was paid £34.15.0. In the 1871 census James Wishart was described as a "master wood carver, employing 2 boys," one being his son James who went on to become a master wood carver in his own right. Among the smaller yards which patronised Wishart were Leckie, Wood & Munro of Torry, by Aberdeen who went into bankruptcy in 1870 owing Wishart £2.9.0, and John Smith of Aberdeen who had a rather bigger bill to meet of £18.11.7 when they ceased operations in 1867. John Duncan who built ships at Kingston near Elgin was another customer of Wishart. His business failed and when the yard closed in 1879 he owed £7.10.0. James Wishart also worked for Alexander Anderson of Forres on the Moray Firth. When this yard failed in 1873 it had an unfinished ship on the stocks and an outstanding bill of £5.11.7½ for carved work.

Wood Carving Company. In the cost books of the Laing yard in Sunderland there are three entries against the Wood Carving Company for wood carvings on steamships. For *Umtali*

64. Dizzie Dunlop 110/78 *portrays the wife or daughter of the owner. The vessel was built in Portmadoc where the carver at the time was Shon Edwards. She was wrecked in 1890 on the Isle of Wight and may be seen in the Maritime Museum at Bembridge.*

64. *'Uncle Johnny' was a member of the family. In fact he was the figurehead from* Tullochgorum 166/67 *a brigantine built by John Duncan of Garmouth and wrecked in 1894. Duncan probably went to Andrew Duncan, the local carver.*

64. *Built in Dundee the brig* Levant 247/53 *was wrecked off Whitby in 1884. It is likely that this figurehead was carved by James Hutton of Dundee. She is preserved in the museum at Whitby and has now been restored.*

64. *This imposing figurehead representing Napoleon III was part of a collection at one time on Burgh Island and is now restored and rests in a museum in Hastings. He came from* Napoleon III 862/55 *built by Barr & Shearer of Ardrossan. and was carved by Archibald Robertson. (Museum of Local History, Hastings)*

2641/96 and *Umvoli 2675/96* they were paid £18.15.0 each and for *Westralia 2884/96* £30.12.3. Nothing more is known about this firm.

Keswick Wood, Maryport. One of the more unusual carvers was Mr. Keswick Wood of Maryport, the proprietor of the K. Wood shipyard. The Cumberland Paquet of 1838 recorded the launch of *Mary 357/39*, a large vessel for the Far East trade. "She has a beautiful full length female figurehead, elaborately carved stern and taffrail, and when we state that they are considered by connoisseurs the ' Chef d'oeuvre ' of the senior Mr. Wood's chisel, we are not aware that stronger commendation could be bestowed upon those rich but chaste specimens of carving in wood." That Mr. Wood was quite an artist is confirmed by a small notebook of his, held by the National Maritime Museum, which carries on every page a sketch or caricature in colour, though oddly enough no sketches of figureheads. There is, however, a sketch of the stern of *Martha 248/38,* and a crest of the Lowther family, presumably for a stern badge. Mr. Wood did not carry out all the carved work as is evident from an entry on his notebook which reads: "29th.April 1839, paid carver £19.0.0 for ship *Carib 328/39."*

John Wynd, Dundee. John Wynd described himself in the Trades Directories for 1840 and 1842 as a "ship carver" but by 1845 this had been changed to "carver and cabinet maker". Wynd carved a figure of Martin Luther for the brig *Luther 249/55* which had been built by the Dundee Shipbuilding Company.

65. *When the counter stern was used it was still possible to apply some form of decoration such as shown below, rope work and 'drops'. This is illustrated in a sketch showing vessels built in about 1853 by Scott's of Greenock. Although of cast metal the original patterns had to be prepared by a ship carver. Scott's specification read "The decorative work on the stern is to be carved in wood, fitted in place, removed, cast in iron and attached using countersunk bolts."*

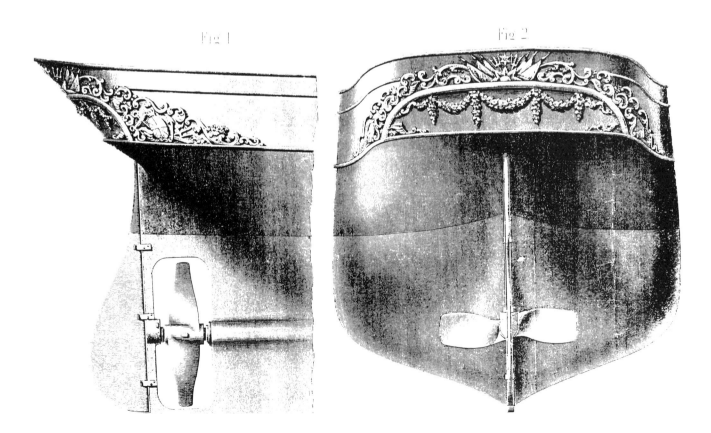

3. Naval Figureheads

66. *This drawing of* Royal George, *a 1st. rate of 100 guns, built at Woolwich in 1756 shows the extensive carved work still permitted on His Majesty's warships. She was decorated under the supervision of Thomas Burrough. (From The Architectural Review.)*

In the Middle Ages the design of warships was such that the stern was more highly decorated than the bow. The ship *Good Pace of the Tower* of 1400 bore on her bows a large golden eagle with a crown in its beak while the stern was decorated with carved figures of St. George, St. Catherine and St. Margaret, emphasising the religious feelings of the day. *Henri Grace a Dieu* of 1488 had a squatting lion as her figurehead, and on the forward bulkhead was a Garter supported by a lion and a dragon, while within the circle of the Garter were the Arms of France and England, quartered and crowned. One hundred years later Sir Walter Raleigh was commenting that ship decorations had become so cumbersome that "the ocean fairly groaned from their weight." The figureheads of the time were still rather insignificant. *Bonaventure* of 47 guns, purchased 1567 had an eagle, *Ark Royal* of 55 guns, built 1587, a mild looking bird, *Mary Rose* of 60 guns, built 1509 carried a unicorn and *Swiftsure* of 41 guns, built 1573, a tiger. Somewhat more complex than these was the figurehead of *White Bear* of 40 guns, built 1563, which was adorned with an image of Jupiter sitting upon an eagle in the clouds. All in all, the Elizabethan warships relied more on painting than carving for decoration.

As the 1600s passed the decoration of warships gained in importance as a matter of prestige. The 100 gun *Royal Sovereign* launched in 1637 was "so gorgeously ornamented with carving and gilding that she seemed to have been designed rather for a vain display of magnificence than for the service of the State." Maybe so, but she remained in service until 1696 when she accidentally caught fire, having been rebuilt twice. Her figurehead was described in detail by Thomas Heywood her designer, "Upon the beak head sitteth Royal King Edgar on horseback trampling upon seven kings. Upon the stem head there is a Cupid, or a child resembling him, bestriding and bridling a lion, which importeth that sufference may curb insolence, and innocence restrain violence; which alludeth to the great mercy of the King, whose mercy is above all his workes. On the bulkhead right forward stand six severall statues in sundry postures; their figures represent Consilium, that is Counsell; Cura, that is Care; Conamen, that is Industry; Counsell holds in her hand a closed or folded scroll; Care a sea compass; Conamen, or Industry a lint stock fired. Upon the other side, to correspond with the former, Vis, which implyeth Force or Strength, holding a sword; Virtus, or Virtue, a sphericall globe; and Victoria, or Victory, a wreath of Lawrell. The moral is that in all high enterprises there ought to be first, Counsell to undertake, then Care to manage and Industry to performe; and in the next place, where there is an Ability and Strength to oppose and Virtue to direct, Victory consequently is always at hand to crown the undertaking."

In 1655 the Protector Cromwell, despite his Puritan beliefs, authorised the building of a new ship with an ornate figurehead similar to that of *Royal Sovereign*. Evelyn wrote in his diary: "I went to see the great ship newly built by the usurper, Oliver, carrying ninety-six brass guns and 1000 tons

67. *This picture of the stern of a Stuart man-o-war, (mid 1600s), shows the elaborate decoration of the time. Prominent are" Ye King's Arms on ye Sterne". (108). (From The Architectural Review)*

67. *The stern of* Boyne, *a 2nd. rate of 98 guns, built in Woolwich in 1790, though less ornate, still required a great deal of carved work. William Burrough was the Master Carver at this time. (From The Architectural Review)*

burthen. In the prow was Oliver on horseback trampling six nations underfoot, a Scot, an Irishman, Dutchman, Frenchman, Spaniard and Englishman, as was easily made out by their several habits. A Fame held a laurel over his insulting head; the words "God with us." This magnificent figurehead was destroyed at the Restoration. Apart from the opulence of the figurehead the sterns of warships were magnificently carved and gilded, while further carving and gilding ran the length of the topsides. In every convenient space were grouped trophies, arms, gods, nymphs and sea monsters (69).
During the 17th. century the cost of decorating warships soared:

White Bear	built 1563, rebuilt 1598	£377
Prince Royal	built 1610	£1309
Prince Royal	rebuilt 1641	£3327 (as rebuilt)
Sovereign of the Seas	built 1637. rebuilt 1660	£6691 (as rebuilt)

These expenditures were on special vessels, and the lion figurehead was commonly used as is shown by numerous references such as "11th. December 1707. The carpenter has been instructed to work on the Lyon on *Mary*, (a 5th. rate, 32 guns, built 1687), which was "very loose upon the knee." Nevertheless the cost of carving and gilding the average warship was still high. It is not surprising to learn that cages of iron bars were fitted around multiple figureheads and the carvings at the corners of the stern. These protected them from damage and also prevented the running rigging from fouling the twists and turns of the carvings. When the royal yacht *Royal Sovereign* of 278 b.m. was launched in 1804 the reporter described the figurehead thus: "It is a representation of Her Majesty with the Imperial Crown over her head. This is encompassed by an iron railing to prevent any injury." In the detailed lists of "ironmongery" supplied to the Naval Dockyards entries are made for "iron bars for the head", presumably to form these cages. In the National Maritime Museum is a shipwright's notebook dated 1684, which is a piece-rate record for building warships. At the end of the book there are several pages devoted to "The cost of furnishing and apparrelling His Majesty's

Ships of War." The carved work required for each rate of warship is detailed and priced. The sums seem incredible by today's standards and so it is fortunate that our shipwright detailed the carved work appropriate to each rate of warship. The following are his entries for each class with the full detail for a 1st. rate vessel:

Rate	Carved work
1st.	£539. 0.0
2nd.	£399.10.0
3rd.	£163.11.0
4th.	£90.11.0
5th.	£46.19.0

Detail for a 1st. rate.(Original spelling used throughout).

Lyon for the head	£40
Ten Head Braketts	18
Two Hair Brackitts	15
Trail board	5
Two Tack Pieces	2.10.0
Two Supports for Catts	12
Rail Heads and Timber Heads	1.10.0
Eight Hanseys	3
Two Figures and Tafferell for ye Entry Ports	12
Two Quarter Pieces	30
A Tafferel	36
Ten Boys for ye Round House Lights	8
King's Arms for ye Sterne	12
Two badges each side of same	14
Balcony on ye Sterne and Ten Brackitts and Badges	25

Ten Bracketts in ye Upper Counter	7
Eight Masque Heads for ye Lower Counter	10
Eight Counter Brackitts Double and Single	6
Two Hanseys for ye Tafferell	8
Eight Doggs upon ye drifts	16
A Belfrey and Supports	8
Ten Bulkhead bracketts for ye Fore Castle	8
Nine Badges for ye same	10
Kings Arms on ye Breast Rails	10
Ten Bulkhead Brackets for ye same rails	8
Nine Badges for ye same	9
Eight Bulkhead Bracketts for ye Round House	6
Fortyfour Round Ports	90
Sixtytwo Royal Garter Stars	31
Six Window Pieces	12
Total	£539

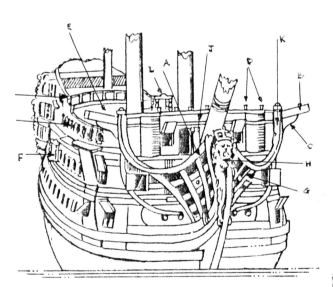

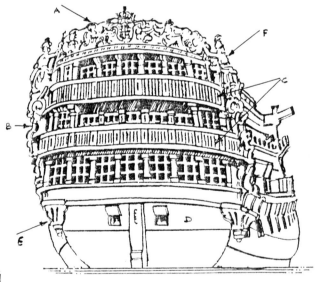

68.

A	Hair brackets	J	Forecastle bulwark
B	Cathead	K	Head rails
C	Cathead bracket	L	Belfry
D	Timber heads	M	Hanseys
E	Round house		
F	Entry port		
G	Head bracket		
H	'Lyon' figurehead		
I	Round gun ports		

68.

A	Taffrail
B	Quarters
C	Balcony
D	Counter
E	Lower finishing
F	Upper finishing

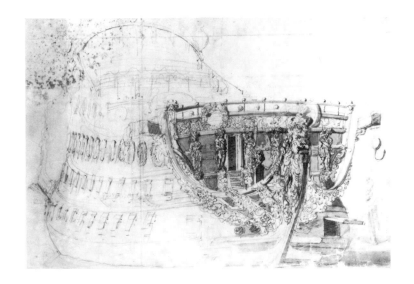

69. *This sketch by Van der Velde of the bows of* Windsor Castle, *a 2nd. rate of 90 guns, built in Woolwich Dockyard in 1678 shows the extravagant carved work of the Stuart period. The Master Carver at this time was John Leadman. (Courtesy of the National Maritime Museum.)*

In 1691 there were the first signs of concern about the cost of carved and gilded work, when the Clerk of the Cheque was instructed to co-operate with the Master Shipwright in checking the quality of the carved work and approving the cost. In 1693 the Storekeeper and the Clerk of the Survey were co-opted to bring up to four the number keeping an eye on costs. In 1699 a warrant was issued directing the Dockyards to "be sparing in the Quantity and Quality of Carved Works and to bring down the Exorbitant Prices." In 1700 another standing order was issued by the Navy Board who had noticed that many vessels had decorative carving internally, much of it on the temporary partitioning which was dismantled when the ship went into action. Costs had again risen and the Navy Board now "prohibited the putting of carved work in cabin coaches and other improper places" and putting "a limitation to the charges of said work." As a guide they introduced a new range of costs to which the dockyards were expected to adhere:

Rate	Previous Limit	Future limit
1st.	£896	£500
2nd.	£420	£300
3rd. 80 guns	£293-164	£150
3rd. 70 guns	£277-160	£130
4th. 60 guns	£157-144	£100
4th. 50 guns	£103-75	£80
5th.	£93-65	£50
6th.	£52-42	£25

69. *"In every convenient space were grouped trophies, arms, gods, nymphs and sea monsters." This picture shows a model of* Eagle, *a 3rd. rate of 64 guns built in 1745 and is reproduced by permission of the National Trust for Scotland, Culzean Castle.*

Finding that simple orders were not enough, the Admiralty, in 1703, issued a warrant detailing the exact degree of decorative work which they were prepared to allow. "The carved works to be reduced to only a Lyon and Trailboard for the Head....the Stern to have only a tafferell and two quarter pieces." The restrictions were not very popular, especially the rule regarding the lion figurehead

70. *This remarkable example of a Lion figurehead, probably about 300 years old, came up for sale in an auction sale room in Torquay. Although only a "Lyon" the detail of the carving is impressive. (By courtesy of Bearne's of Torquay.)*

70. *This Lion from* Barfleur *is usually credited to one built in 1768. However the "couchant" posture is not reconcilable with the bow of the period and in any case it can be seen in photographs of the battleship built in 1892 of 10,500 tons.*

and in 1727 the Admiralty relented and allowed the use of a figure even on smaller ships. In 1737 they changed their minds again and issued a schedule to limit the prices allowed for carved work for various classes of warship, specifying the "Lyon" as the figurehead.

Guns	Lyon	Trailboard	Tafferell	Quarter pieces	Total
100	£44 . 8.0	£7 . 4.0	£55 . 8.0	£57.12.0	£166.12.0
90	39 .0.0	5 . 6.0	45 . 0.0.	47 . 8.0	136.14.0
80	31.14.0	4 . 5.0	38.16.0.	40. 0.0	114.15.0
70	23.18.0.	2.16.2.	30.18.0.	30 . 4.0.	87.16.2
50	13 .2.0	2 . 1.5	16 . 4.0	16 . 4.0	47 .4.5
40	10 .2.0	1.13.4	12 . 7.0	13 . 0.0	37 .2.4
20	7 .4.0	1 . 4.8	9 . 8.0	10 .7.0	28 .3.8

In about 1737 a Frenchman reported that the carved work on English ships was excessive and crudely executed. Unfortunately none of these remarkable multiple figureheads have survived and there are only two sternboards which can be examined to see if his criticism was justified, *Royal Charles* 80 gun ship of 1655 in Holland and *Association* 2nd. rate, 90 guns of 1697, in Penzance (108). In 1773 the Admiralty relented once more and officially approved the use of figures. They had in fact been carved and fitted despite the 1703 order. In conjunction with this new order a new schedule of costs was issued:

Prices allowed for carving the Heads of His Majesty's Ships.

100 guns	Double head	£100. 0. 0
90 guns	Double head	85. 0. 0
74 guns	Single figure enriched	32. 0. 0
64 guns	Single figure enriched	25. 0. 0

Other carving costs to remain the same.

(New classes of ship had been introduced and although they were to be permitted to have figures, these were not to cost more than the "Lyon" as previously specified for the nearest class in the 1737 list. The new classes were 50, 44, 32, 28 and 24 guns).

The Dockyards were further urged to make carvings "as light as possible" and to "use the most durable wood". None of the regulations seem to have been complied with when *Victory* 1st. rate, 100 guns was built and launched in 1765 as the carver's specification for the decorative work was very detailed and occupied 120 lines of writing.

The Admiralty Office changed their minds again in 1796, sternly directing the Dockyards to "explode" carved work aboard His Majesty's ship, both on those being built and those under repair. This invoked a panic in the dockyards where they were repairing war damaged vessels. Plymouth had *Magnificent* 3rd. rate, 74 guns of 1766 in for repair and only by assuring the Navy Board that the repairs were small were they permitted to go ahead. Even the 1796 order did not satisfy the Admiralty as in the following year, worried in case the dockyards were not complying, their Lordships "directed and required the yards to submit designs for the Heads and Sterns, similar to a design which they would issue." In 1799 another order instructed that an estimate should accompany the sketch. The Dockyards must have tried to by-pass these orders as reminders were issued in 1806. An 1809 order pointed out that extra carved work would not be paid for, an order which was repeated in 1812. Each year that followed found fresh orders, restrictions and permissible designs coming out. In 1815 a revised schedule of allowable costs reached the yards.

Guns	Figurehead	Tafferell & Quarters	Upper Finishing	Lower Finishing	Total
100-120	£50	£40. 0.0	£4. 0.0	£6. 0.0	£100 . 0.0
90	35	37.10.0	3.15.0	5.10.0	81.15.0
80	21	21. 0.0	3. 5.0	3.15.0	49 . 0 0
74	21	16.14.0	3. 3.0	3.10.0	44 . 7.0
50	6	13. 0.0	3 . 0.0	3. 0.0	25. 0.0
36-38	6	10.10.0	2.10.0	2. 5.0	21. 5.0
32	6	8.10.0	2.10.0	2. 5.0	19. 5.0
20-24	6	7 .0.0	2 .7.0	2. 3.0	17.10.0

As late as 1832 the Admiralty was still sending out reminders that they wished to inspect and approve all designs and estimates before the ship carvers commenced work on any warship. The Lion was never really adopted as the figurehead on large warships which generally had an image on the bow representing the vessel's name. Where appropriate a lion head would be used as on the *Lion,* a 2nd. rate of 80 guns launched in 1847, where the figurehead was of that noble beast, but of a design based on the Lion Rampant of Scotland. It has been suggested that the design had come down through a series of warships named *Lion* from the first of the name captured from the Scots in 1511 when Lord Thomas Howard defeated the famous Scottish captain Sir Andrew Barton.

In the early days the decorative work was carried out by outside contractors who were appointed as Master Carvers and provided with facilities within the dockyard. It would appear that the ship carvers considered themselves superior to the shipwrights and they had their own workshops adjacent to the mould shop. The employment of ship carvers within the dockyard ceased around 1815, a fact which seems to have taken some time to register with the Navy Board, who, ever conscious of the cost of carved work, kept challenging the Superintendents of the Dockyards for using the services of outside contractors-"Why do you wish to employ Mr. Hall when there are carvers on your establishment ?", only to be advised that: "No carvers are now employed at the Yard." In December 1833 the Superintendent of each yard was once more instructed to submit designs and estimates for all carved work required for ships being built or repaired in their yard for approval by their Lordships, prior to an order being placed with the carver. This resulted in a flood of paperwork and much of the original correspondence has been preserved for the period 1832 to 1860 including carvers' quotations and sketches. The procedure was as follows:

Superintendent to carver: a plan of the stem and stern of the vessel.

Carver to Superintendent: the plan with a sketch of the figurehead and decorative work superimposed, and an estimate.

Superintendent to Admiralty: sketch and estimate.

Admiralty to Superintendent: approval, possibly with modifications, instructions to issue the block of yellow pine to the carver.

Superintendent to carver: order to proceed and instruction regarding the delivery of the finished figurehead.

Things did not always go smoothly. In 1833 the Surveyor to the Navy issued an instruction that a block of yellow pine be sent to Robert Hall to be converted into a figurehead, but before the block was sent off the order was rescinded because another carver was already engaged for the work. In 1854 the system came to a standstill when the yards ran out of yellow pine. Portsmouth needed the timber for *Marlborough* 1st. rate, 121 guns, a screw vessel launched 1855, but when they applied to Woolwich for help they had run out as well. Devonport were looking for yellow pine for the figurehead of *Imperieuse* a screw frigate of 2,358 b.m., launched 1852 and they went to Woolwich only to be disappointed. Two years later Woolwich had run out once more while Deptford's store of the timber was entirely exhausted.

The civil servants in the Admiralty kept a close eye on the costs continually comparing prices for similar figureheads from the various carvers and asking for reductions where appropriate. Several times they reminded Superintendents on the south coast that carvers were to be paid according to the prices paid to "eastern yards". In 1843 when the Hellyers put in an invoice for £916. 9.0 for work done on the Royal Yacht *Victoria & Albert,* a wooden paddle vessel of 1,034 bm., a cost which represented only part of the contract, their bill was questioned and they were pressurised into reducing it to £832.12.6. In 1850 Nehemiah Williams sent to the Admiralty a price list which obviously undercut the Hellyers. This was passed to Portsmouth Dockyard for comment and they indicated that Hellyers' prices were reasonable for the quality of workmanship achieved. Sensing loss of business the Hellyers stated that they could match Williams' prices but that inferior work would result. J. E. Hellyer lowered his prices but regretted the resultant fall off in quality after 55 years of giving satisfaction.

Although most of the 19th. century was a time of peace there was plenty of work for the carvers replacing figureheads which had decayed. In 1851 new figureheads were required for *St. Vincent,* a 1st. rate, 120 guns, of 1815 and *Nile,* 2nd. rate, 92 guns, of 1839, and in the following year two wooden paddle sloops, *Phoenix* of 1832, 802 b.m. and *Vesuvius* of 1839, 970 b.m. both received new heads. Figureheads were lost in collision or carried away by rough seas. *Bee* of 1842, which was an experimental vessel with both screw and paddles, lost hers almost on her maiden voyage as did *Basilisk* of 1848, a wooden paddle sloop of 1,031 b.m. *Virago* wooden paddle sloop of 1842, and the wooden screw sloops *Racoon* of 1857, 1,467 b.m. and *Rinaldo* of 1860, 1,365 b.m., lost their figureheads in collisions in their first year in service. Repairs were a continuing source of income for the carvers. The Royal Yacht *Fairy* of 1845, an iron screw vessel of 312 b.m. needed repairs in 1848 to the figurehead, the royal arms on the stern, the carved work on the quarter-deck, and to the cable moulding round the hull. From time to time the Admiralty changed the name of a vessel. *Tremendous* 3rd. rate, 74 guns, of 1784 was renamed *Grampus* in 1845. She had already had a new figurehead fitted in 1810 carved by George Williams. The Hellyers were instructed to provide a replacement in 1845 for which they carved a bust of Hercules. The carver had only just finished when he was requested to alter the figurehead of Hercules to suit the new name, which he did, the new bust representing Neptune. The figure of James Watt was put in store when *Watt* a wooden paddle frigate of 1,641 b.m. was rechristened *Retribution* in 1844 and was brought out again in 1853 when *James Watt,* 2nd. rate, 80 guns, was built. In 1839 *Royal Frederick,* 1st. rate, 110 guns, was renamed *Queen* and Hellyer was instructed to carry out alterations to the original figure. Before *Repulse* 2nd. rate screw vessel 91 guns, went into service in 1855 she was renamed *Victor Emmanuel* and given a new figurehead. The old one was kept until 1861 when it was altered and fitted to *Defiance,* 2nd. rate screw vessel, 81 guns. On several occasions when a figurehead was required for a warship named after a famous person the Admiralty would commission a sculptor to provide a bust as a guide for the carver. A Mr. S. F. B. Hayden supplied a bust of Nelson for *Trafalgar*, 1st. rate, 110 guns, of 1841 and a bust of Sir John Graham for *Cumberland*, 3rd. rate, 70 guns, of 1842.

Although the ram bow was introduced the Navy still wanted its figureheads. At first these were indeed figures on the bow with complicated designs worked back along the hull, but later the figure was abandoned and only the intricate designs remained. However warships with clipper bows were still being built and true figureheads were still being fitted. *Cadmus 1,070/03*, a sloop built in Sheerness Dockyard was the last warship to have a figurehead.

The figureheads on warships were sometimes painted in colour, sometimes white. When the figurehead for the 1st. rate, 120 gun *Nelson* was completed in 1814, the Admiralty suggested that it would "in their opinion appear more to advantage by being properly painted in colours than by plain white." They were kept smart and each time the vessel was painted the carvings on the head, stern and galleries were "refreshed." When *Dorsetshire* of 1694, 3rd. rate, 80 guns, received this treatment in 1717 the cost was £4.10.0. The operation of gilding was undertaken by the company which painted the ship as is evident from the accounts rendered. The sailors were proud of their colourful figureheads and a legend has been handed down that, aboard a warship which was constantly slow in their sail drill, the exasperated captain declared: "Now I'll tell you what my lads, unless you are off those yards and the sails hoisted again before any other ship in the squadron, by the Lord Harry, I'll paint your figurehead black!" At the next sail drill his frigate led the rest.

73. *For each vessel the Admiralty issued a 'carving sketch' which showed the carver the dimensions of the timbers on which the figurehead was to be mounted and the clearance below the bowsprit. This is Hellyer's sketch for* Myrmidon *a wood screw survey vessel of 697 tons. b.m. built in Chatham in 1867. (A Myrmidon is defined as a ruffian fighting for a daring leader).*
(Public Record Office. ADM 87/77)

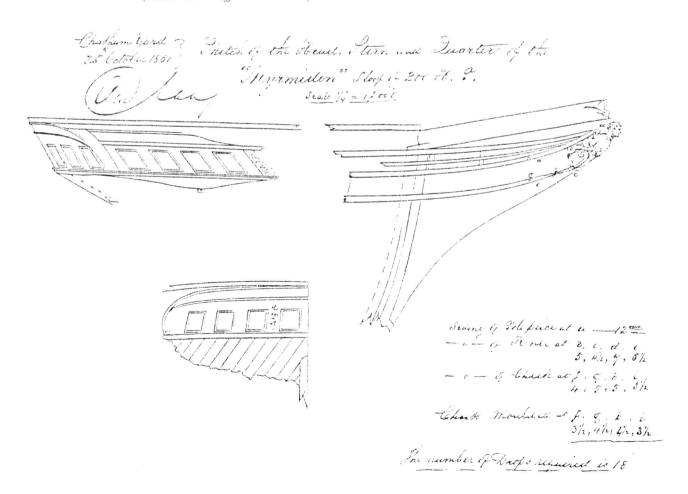

4. Carvers to the Naval Dockyards

74. *In 1979 a painting was sold in a Torquay auction house which captures the atmosphere of the workshop of a carver of naval figureheads in the 18th century. (Courtesy Sotherby, Bearne of Torquay)*

Anthony Allen, Plymouth. Anthony Allen worked for the Plymouth yard between 1691 and 1701. Only the records of the later years give detail, showing that he was doing a lot of repair work, from *Jolly* a 10 gun sloop, captured from the French in 1693 for which he was paid £1.14.0, to £9.10.0 for *Chester* of 1691, a 4th. rate, 48 gun vessel. In 1698, he cut the complete carved work for the new-building *Carlisle*, a 4th. rate, 48 gun ship, at £100.19.0. She blew up in 1700. In 1700 he completed work on the newly built 4 gun yacht *St. Looe* at a cost of £24.19.6. Every now and again there was a heavy expenditure for which there is no apparent reason. *Medway*, a 4th. rate of 60 guns had work carried out on her in 1700 which was valued at £32.5.0, yet she was only built in 1693 and was not rebuilt until 1718. In 1701 Anthony Allen died and the final payment was made to his widow Sarah.

Lewis Allen, (sometimes spelt Allin or Allon), Portsmouth. (75). Lewis Allen is first mentioned in 1670 when he presented a bill for £24.1.6 for work done on *Gloucester*, a 54 gun vessel built in 1654. For the next few years he was kept busy with repairs to warship decoration, sometimes at a quite a cost. *York*, another 54 gun ship built in 1654 was refurbished for £54.4.6 in 1671. The navy purchased *Eagle* in 1672, fitted her out as a fire ship with £ 23.11.0 of carved work, only for her to sink in 1673. During the war with the Dutch from 1672 until 1674 three ships received his attention after the Battle of Solebay in May 1672, the 32 gun *Tiger* of 1647, the 54 gun *Gloucester* of 1654 and the 70 gun *Resolution* of 1667, the last being quite expensive at £ 20.18.0. In 1676 the navy embarked on a programme of expansion and sanctioned the construction of thirty new vessels. This was a period when extensive decorative carved work was still permitted and Lewis Allen was the carver who undertook the work at Portsmouth. Among them were the 3rd. rate, 70 gun *Eagle* of 1679 which cost £160, the 2nd. rate 90 gun *Vanguard* of 1678, £105, and *Ossory*, another 2nd rate, built in 1682 which cost £141.2.0.

In 1684 Samuel Pepys took office as Secretary for the Affairs of the Admiralty of England and found Naval affairs in an appalling state. His agents reported to him in 1685 that out of 175 ships in the Fleet, only 33 were fit for service, many of the others being too rotten to move from their moorings. He instituted a programme of repair calculated to take from 1686 until 1688, a programme which was reflected in the amount of carved work required.

Royal Charles	1st. rate, 100 guns.	built 1673	£86.18.0.
Warspite	3rd. rate, 70 guns.	built 1666	£130. 2.0.
Royal James	1st. rate, 100 guns.	built 1675	£54. 0. 0.

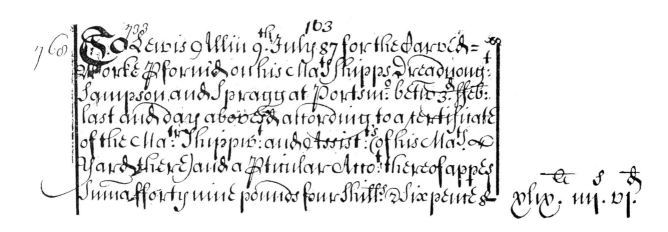

75. *The clerk in the Admiralty laboriously copied out every item of expenditure in full detail and in an elegant script. The above was his entry for one of the contracts with Lewis Allin which read: "To Lewis Allin 9th. July 1687 for the carved worke performed on His Majesty's Shipps* Dreadnought, Sampson *and* Spragge *at Portsmouth between 3rd. February last and day above and according to a certificate of the Master Shipwright and Assistant of His Majesty's Yard there and a particular account thereof appears suma Forty-nine Pounds four shillings and sixpence."*
(Dreadnought *62 guns, built 1654,* Sampson *12 gun fire ship, purchased 1678 and* Sprague *a fire ship.)*
(Public Record Office ADM 20/45)

    The programme also included new ships:

20th.July 1692	2nd. rate, 80 guns	*Russell*	£172
30th.Sept.1692	2nd. rate, 80 guns	*Russell*	£5
20th.March 1695	2nd. rate, 80 guns	*Shrewsbury*	£269.4.0.

The second entry for *Russell* was detailed: "a large piece on the Top of the Taffrail 17 ft. long and one ft. broad, cut with 2 large Dragons lying -£2, Eight Ports for ye Forecastle cut with Cherubims, Fruit and Flowers-£3".

    A typical entry in the Accountant General's ledgers read:
"To Lewis Allin 30th Nov. 1687 for price of severall carved workes by him performed on His Majesty's Shipp *Warspite* at Portsmouth between 21st. April last and day above and according to the Master Shipwright and his Assistant, their certificate together with a particular account thereof remaining in the Navy Office appears suma. One Hundred Thirty pounds and two shillings."
(*Warspite* was a 3rd. rate, 70 gun ship, built in 1666).

    During his tenure as Master Carver, England was at war with France from 1689 to 1697 and with France and Spain in the War of the Spanish Succession from 1702 to 1713. For a time the ledger entries gave no detail but in 1702 the practice of recording the names of the ships was resumed. After the battle of Vigo at least eleven of the warships which took part passed through Allen's hands, the highest cost being for *Eagle*, a 3rd. rate, 70 guns, built in 1679 on which £16.4.6. was spent. Rebuilding brought in money as well. When *Elizabeth*, of 1679 a 3rd. rate of 70 guns was rebuilt in 1704 she was refurbished at a price of £40.1.6, only to be captured by the French in November 1704, before the bill had even been paid. Two of his last big contracts were for running repairs costing £31.15.0 on a 3rd. rate, 80 gun ship *Cumberland*, built in 1695, and £24.4.0 for *Sunderland*, a 4th. rate of 60 guns, built in 1695, both carried out in 1704. In 1705 he died and final payments were made to his executors.

    Robert Brown, Southampton. In 1414 a 6 gun ship called *Holigost* was launched by Soper in Southampton. The carver Robert Brown was paid £4.13.4 for the cost of timber for, and the carving of, a swan and an antelope for the vessel.

    Thomas Burrough, Deptford & Woolwich, (66). Shortly after the outbreak of the War of the Austrian Succession in 1740, a war which lasted until 1748, Thomas Burrough started working at Woolwich and Deptford, carrying out repairs, sometimes extensive and costly. The bomb *Furnace* of 1740, a 12 gun vessel cost only 10/- while *Lennox* of 1678, a 3rd.rate 70 guns, required an expenditure of £34.4.2. His first new-building was in 1745, *Devonshire*, a 3rd. rate 74 guns for which he received £114.15.0, followed in 1748 by *Lancaster* a 3rd. rate 66 guns , similarly priced. Over a two year period 6th. March 1749 to 29th. April 1751 he must have been kept very busy as he received a payment of £1538.2.5. This would have included the cost of the decorative carving on the yacht *Royal Caroline* of 1749 which came to the incredible sum of £ 1100.11.0. This was not all, as the gold leaf which was applied to her carved work took 120,000 leaves of gold which cost the Navy £950.13.11. She was thus more expensively gilded than her predecessor of the same name, built in 1700 and rebuilt in 1733, on which a mere 60,825 leaves of gold were applied at a cost of £456.3.9 on the yacht, and £26.16.3. on the ship's boat. A slightly less costly royal yacht was *Dorset* of 1753, rated at 10 guns, for which Burrough received £531.7.1. A sloop of 8 guns such as *Cruizer* of 1752 was worth £21.9.0.

Normally the accounts clerk entered only the name of the vessel and the sum paid out, but in 1755 he gave a detailed account of the work on which the money had been spent, including the decorative work for *Cambridge*, a 3rd. rate 80 guns launched at Deptford in 1755. As specifications for carved work for this period are rare it is worth quoting the entry in full:

"The head piece in front the bust of His Majesty proper and two Boys each supporting the Royal Motto and two winds blowing forward under the Royal Bust, and Neptune on a seahorse holding his Trident, with the other hand supports a large leather-work shield. In front St. George proper in it, together with scrowls, foliage and Grotesques. £70.0.0

The Trail Boards cut Birds, Fish and Sea Weeds 4.5.0

The Taffrail, in the middle the figure Mars holding a sword and Laurel branch leaning on a shield supported by a Boy, a cock in trophies of war, on one side is Minerva with her proper Attributes and a Boy holding her shield, on the other side is Appollo with his Attributes, proper and the lower rail with raking leaves and Grotesques £38.16.0

The Quarter pieces, on one side is Jupiter, also Mercury each with their proper Attributes, on the top a Boy supporting the Royal Globe with a palm branch, on the other side Juno and Valour, each with their proper Attributes, on the top a boy with fish and sea weeds, together with scrowls and foliage £ 40.0.0

A large piece to the larboard quarter piece cut a truss scrowl with a Lyon's head and paws supporting a shield with the Royal letters in it £ 3.10.0

A piece of drapery to the quarter piece and new working over all the after part of the scarph and part of the figure and body and thigh part of the eagle's wings £ 1.17.6"

In the following year *Deal Castle*, a 6th. rate 20 guns was launched at Blackwall and she too was well endowed with carving:

"The head, cut a Roman figure representing Mars drawing his sword £7 .4 .0

The taffrail, in the middle the bust of Pallas with her proper attributes together with rich trophies of war on one side a Genius representing Navigation proper, on the other Astronomy, at each end a Dragon £ 9.8.0

The quarterpieces, each a Term Boy with scrowls, foliage and grotesques £10.7.0

The trail boards, cut fish and seaweeds £ 1.4.0"

In 1756 he completed the carved work for *Royal George*, a 1st. rate, 100 gun ship built at Woolwich. This vessel must have been something special as the Admiralty lavished £424.7.0 on her decoration, instead of their supposedly strict limit of £166.12.0. In 1756 the Seven Years War began and Burrough was again busy with repairs with the occasional re-construction which involved more expensive work by him. In 1757 *Princess Amelia*, a 3rd. rate of 80 guns was built with carved work costing £110.10.0, just within the statuary figure of £114.15.0 Again, despite the war, the royal yachts received regular attention and seldom cheaply. *Fubbs* of 1682 appeared frequently in the accounts. One of the new vessels for which Burrough carved was *Hercules*, a 3rd. rate 74 guns which brought him £63.18.2 in 1759. About this time the detailing of the accounts was curtailed and only totals of cash paid were entered.

In 1771 the Board issued a warrant stating that Thomas Burrough was appointed Master Carver for Woolwich and Deptford yards. Since Thomas Burrough had already been Master Carver for 28 years we might assume that his son was being appointed in his place. In 1775 England went to war again, this time against the Americans who were fighting for their independence. Seeing a chance to catch the British fleet at a disadvantage the French declared war in 1778. The last entry traced for Thomas Burrough was 1788.

Between 1757 and 1788, while Thomas Burrough was Master Carver at Deptford the 'front line 'strength of the fleet was increased with the launching of three 64 gun ships, nineteen 74's, one 98 gun, the last being *Impregnable* in 1786. At Woolwich they built one 60 gun ship, five 64's, six 74's, two 90's and the 98 gun *Prince* of 1788.

William Montague Burrough, Deptford & Woolwich. (67, 78).   When he took over in 1790 William Burrough had a busy first five months in Woolwich occupied on six ships, two with new work and four requiring remedial carving. The new ships were *Boyne*, a 98 gun 2nd. rate and *Martin*, a 16 gun brig sloop, while the other included *Niger* a 5th. rate of 38 guns, built in 1759. After Whitfield and Keast were appointed at Deptford in 1797 Burrough's work became confined to Woolwich. There was a programme of modernisation in 1801 which saw the launching at Woolwich of eight 74's, together with two 98's and the 120 gun ship *Nelson*. Although in 1804 the yard seems to have cancelled his official appointment as contract carver they continued to use him. In 1805 *Ocean* a 2nd. rate of 98 guns was built and was given a figurehead representing Neptune. With the war against Napoleon in progress he must have been dealing with battle damage. Not only that, but maintaining the continuous and tight blockade of the French ports, especially Brest, in all kinds of weather must have called for a great deal of repair work. One entry stands out among the others. In 1805, months before the Battle of Trafalgar, there was a payment of £1,627.6.1, a lot of money for carved work even in those days. In 1806 the officers in charge of the yard also brought in John Grayfoot. Between them the two carvers executed carved work for several new warships, *Invincible*, 1809, *San Domingo* 1809, both 3rd. rate 74's, and *Undaunted, Manilla* and *Leda*, all 5th. rates of 38 guns launched in 1809. The payments were made to Burrough & Co. and it would seem as though Burrough and Grayfoot were working in partnership.

Among the stories which abound about figureheads is one about *Brunswick*, a 3rd. rate of 74 guns, built in Deptford in 1790. During the battle of The Glorious First of June, while *Brunswick* was engaged with the French *Vengeur*, a shot from *Vengeur* carried away the hat of the British ship's figurehead, the Duke of Brunswick. Immediately word was passed aft and the captain sent forward his spare cocked hat to be set upon the figurehead so that:
> "The noble Duke came through it
> Like a fighter born and bred,
> With his hand upon his sword hilt
> And his hat upon his head."

No payments were recorded to Burrough & Co. after 1810.

Jeremiah Carraway, Chatham.   In January 1797 Jeremiah Carraway, a journeyman ship carver, petitioned the Admiralty for work. He had been working in the naval yard at Chatham but had been laid off due to shortage of orders for carved work. He was pleading to be taken on to the yard's pay books as a labourer.

Chichley.   The Chichley family were carvers for Chatham and Sheerness from 1713 until 1777. Their 'history' is rather complicated and is best summarised as follows:

1713-1737   Richard Chichley, Chatham and Sheerness.
1737-1743   Abigail Chichley, Chatham.
1740-1743   Abigail and Richard Chichley, Sheerness.
1744-1760   Richard Chichley, Chatham and Sheerness.

78. *This immense figure came from* Ocean, *a 2nd. rate of 98 guns, built in Woolwich in 1805 where William Burrough was Master Carver. Once preserved on the sea wall at Sheerness this carving decayed. (Craig/Farr collection.)*

78. Foudroyant *was a 2nd rate of 80 guns, built in 1798 at Plymouth. This figurehead however was a new one carved by James Dickerson in 1817. Although only a bust the huge size is indicated by the figures of the two children standing beside him. (Taken at Chepstow by Lt. Cmdr. Moreland.)*

1764-1765   Richard and Elizabeth Chichley, Sheerness.

1765-1766   Richard and Elizabeth Chichley and William Savage, Chatham and Sheerness.

1767-1770   Richard and Elizabeth Chichley, Sheerness and Deptford.

1770-1777   Elizabeth Chichley and William Savage, Chatham and Sheerness.

Abigail Chichley, Chatham & Sheerness.   Payments were made to Abigail Chichley for carved work performed at Chatham and Sheerness over a period 1739 to 1743. Most was remedial, sometimes quite extensive judging from the costs involved. *Orford*, of 1698, a 3rd. rate, 70 guns, cost £30.4.0, *Barfleur*, of 1697, 2nd. rate, 80 guns, £61.18.0, *Cornwall* of 1692, a 2nd. rate, 80 guns, £86.7.0. From time to time new work was required including *Chatham Yacht* of 1741, 6 guns, £49.19.6, and *Stirling Castle*, 3rd. rate, 70 guns, built in 1742 at Chatham, £87.16.2.

Richard Chichley, Chatham & Sheerness. (80).   Although during most of his time as Master Carver this country was at peace, there was a steady flow of work. Between 1713 and 1716 he repaired 29 vessels issuing bills from 10/- to £52.0.0. From 1716 to 1720 there were 73 vessels from 3/6 to £82.0.0. Several warships were rebuilt attracting a great deal of work. 1717, *Newark*, 2nd. rate, 80 guns, of 1695, £34.12.0. 1719, *Swallow*, 4th. rate, 54 guns, of 1703, £30.15.0 and 1718, *Queenborough*, yacht of 1671, £24.7.0. The rebuilding of *London*, 96 guns, of 1666, in 1721 was more expensive at £116.0.0, as was that of the *Union* in 1725 when she was redecorated for £120.10.0. She had originally been built in 1680 as *Albermarle*, a 2nd. rate, of 90 guns.

The accounts clerk occasionally put in a bit of detail of the work done. For example in 1719: *Chester*, a 4th. rate, of 50 guns, built in 1708.

A Lyon for the head, cut very rich	£10. 0. 0
A Taffrail for the Stern	10. 0. 0
A Trailboard for the Head	1.15. 0

Two quarter pieces for the Stern   9. 0. 0
Nassau, a 3rd. rate of 70 guns, built in 1706.
        A Lyon for the head, cut very rich   £14. 0. 0
        A Trailboard for the same, cut into two parts   2. 5. 0

One of the vessels on which Chichley worked was *Pembroke,* a 4th. rate, 60 gun, built in 1733 which foundered in 1745, was raised and redecorated at a cost of £58.8.0. In 1739 fighting broke out against Spain in the War of Jenkin's Ear, followed in 1740 by the War of the Austrian Succession when the French allied themselves with Spain, a conflict which lasted until 1748. In that year *Somerset* was launched, a 3rd. rate 64 guns which earned Chichley £87.16.2, while on the same account were repairs to *Cumberland,* a 3rd. rate 80 guns built in 1710 reduced to 66 guns, costing £114.5.0, almost the cost for a new vessel. In 1756 another *Union* was built, again a 2nd. rate of 90 guns and she was decorated with carved work amounting to £136.14.0, exactly the permitted amount.

Chichley had several new warships to his credit. *Niger,* a 5th. rate of 32 guns, built in Sheerness in 1759, £37.2.4. *Valiant* of 1759, and *Bellona* of 1760, both 3rd. rates on 74 guns, built in Chatham each decorated at a cost of £87.16.2. A curious entry in 1760 was the spending of £90.11.0 on *Centaur,* a 6th. rate 24 gun, of 1746, before selling her in 1761.

Between 1767 and 1768 Richard and Elizabeth Chichley assisted Thomas Burrough at Deptford, receiving £299.7.11 for their efforts.

Elizabeth Chichley, Chatham & Sheerness.   Elizabeth Chichley was partner to both Richard Chichley and William Savage and her work is covered under their names.

Gerrard (Garrett) Christmas, Woolwich.   When the 41 gun ship *Merhonour* of 1590 was rebuilt in 1615 at Woolwich, among the items that were fitted was a stern lantern with carved work by Garrett Christmas, decorated with "seven tearmes, seven cartrooses, seven fishes and one Lyon", all for £2.0.0. When *Sovereign of the Seas,* a 100 gun ship was launched at Woolwich in 1637 she was the most heavily embellished warship of her time. Much of the decoration was designed by Thomas Heywood and Sir Anthony van Dyck, the carved work being executed under the supervision of Gerrard Christmas. The name of Gerrard Christmas appears when he was working on ships being built at Harwich during 1666-1668 .The records were badly written in old script and most of the entries are indecipherable. One which is clear relates to *Francis,* a 6th. rate of 16 guns

79. *The 5th. rate, 40 gun* Acasta *was built in 1797, but in 1810 her stern work was found to be damaged and James Dickerson was instructed to cut new carved work. Compared with the sterns on page 67 this one in a little less ornate. (Public Record Office ADM 106.)*

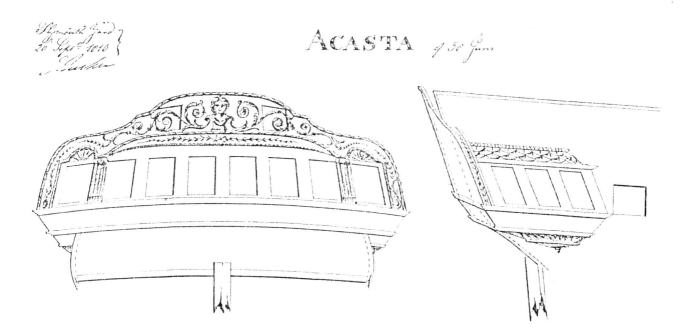

which was decorated at a cost of £300 in 1666. All other payments made in that year were for small amounts between £10 and £20. Another refers to *Resolution*, a 3rd. rate, 70 gun ship launched in 1667.

There were other members of the family engaged in ship carving and their names are recorded against warships being built in 1666. James Christmas worked on *Rupert*, a 3rd. rate, 66 gun vessel built at Harwich, while William Christmas was responsible for *Warspite*, a 3rd. rate, 70 gun ship launched at a civilian yard at Blackwall.

Henry Christmas, Kinsale. Faced with the ever present threat of a French invasion of Ireland the Navy maintained a dockyard at Kinsale. Between 1696 and 1700 they also had a Master Carver by the name of Henry Christmas. The accounts clerk made lengthy entries but the sums of money were small. For *Speedwell*, an 8 gun fire ship built in 1690 "a Belfry with Sea Lyons and an enrichment on the rails," the price was a mere 8/-, while for *Transporter Lighter*, a 7 gun ketch built in 1677 "a Quarter Piece wrought with a boy and a dart in his hand, treading on a fish, with a scrowle and leafe 5' 9" long, two @ 2/6", a total of 5/-. Henry Christmas worked on *Medway*, a

80. *The figurehead of* Elizabeth *is reputed to have come from a 3rd. rate 70 gun ship built in 1706. She was rebuilt in 1737 and possibly saw service with the East India Company. This figurehead is not the original but one carved by Richard Chichley for the 1737 rebuild. (From the Craig/Farr collection)*

4th. rate of 48 guns, captured from the French in 1697 and when *Kinsale*, a 5th. rate of 32 guns was built in Kinsale in 1700 her carved work cost £22.0.0.

Richard Cord, Bristol. When the Navy was expanded in 1666 by the construction of new vessels, two were ordered to be built in the West country. *St. David*, a 4th. rate, 54 gun ship was completed at a new yard at Lydney in 1667, while *St. Patrick*, a 4th. rate, 48 gun ship was built in Bristol. The master carver responsible for their decoration was Richard Cord.

Thomas Coward, Portsmouth. In 1698 Thomas Coward received payment for "Sundry carved workes by him performed upon several of his Majesty's shippes at Portsmouth between May 1696 and June 1697, for the sume of £387.1.2." This was almost enough to decorate a 2nd. rate.

Thomas Davidson (Davison), Deptford. Thomas Davidson's name first appears in 1700 when he was taken into partnership at Chatham by Joseph Wymhurst along with John Carter. One of their first jobs was *Dartmouth* a 4th. rate of 48 guns, built in 1693, captured by the French in 1695 and recaptured in 1702 when the War of the Spanish Succession began. The three carvers refurbished her for £27.10.0 but their artistic efforts were lost when she was wrecked in 1703. Another and more important contract was the work on *Britannia*, along with Matthias Fletcher. She was a 1st. rate of 100 guns launched in 1682 and although it was not recorded as a 'rebuild', the Admiralty paid out £172.6.8 to the partners and £328.14.7 to Fletcher for new carved work. In 1703, after several well-paying orders, the partnership was dissolved. Later, in 1710, Thomas Davidson and John Carter were installed as Master Carvers at Deptford until Carter died in 1712 leaving Davidson on his own until 1715. Most of his income was from fairly small repairs, but it was enlivened by large payments for work on the Royal yachts which included in 1713, £121.5.11½ for *Fubbs* of 1682, £220.10.2½ for *Mary* of 1660, and £169.6.5½ for *William and Mary* of 1694.

81. *This magnificent figure has stood for many years at the entrance to Portsmouth harbour and came from* Royal William, *a 1st. rate of 120 guns., built in 1833. This figurehead was carved by Frederick Dickerson when the vessel was rebuilt in 1860 as a 72 gun screw steamship. The cost was only £35. (Courtesy John Smith)*

81. *This 12 foot high image of Lord Anson was carved by J. E. & J. Hellyer for the 91 gun screw ship* Anson *built at Woolwich in 1860. A globe is incorporated in the design in memory of the famous round the world voyage. (Courtesy Royal Navy, Chatham)*

81. *Robert Hall carved this figurehead for* Cleopatra, *a 6th. rate of 26 guns, built in Pembroke Dock in 1835. His interpretation of the Egyptian queen is not very convincing. (Courtesy Royal Navy, H.M.S. Ganges, Shotley)*

81. *In 1822, during the tenure of George Williams as the carving contractor for Chatham,* Diana, *a 5th. rate of 46 guns was built. It is hard to associate this stolid figure with the Goddess of the hunt. (Courtesy Royal Navy, Chatham)*

82. *The ledgers of the Accountant General were huge affairs measuring about 17" x 12" and the above extract has been reduced to a quarter of its original area. For each payment the clerk had to write out the same wording with only the names and the sum of money changed. The above reads "To Matthias Ffletcher 30th. April 1687 for ye carved worke performed on His Majesty's Shipps* Dover, Crowne, Fforesight *and* Greenwich *at Deptford betweene 1st. January last and day above according to certificate of the Master Shipwright of His Majesty's yard there and a particular Account thereof remaining in Navy Office appears suma Ffiftyfour pounds thirteen shillings and sixpence."*
(Dover, 45 guns, built 1654, Crowne, 48 guns built 1654 as Taunton, Foresight, *50 guns, built 1650 and* Greenwich, *a 4th. rate of 54 guns, built 1666). (Public Record Office ADM 20/45)*

One of his last jobs was *Rochester,* a 48 gun ship, built in 1693 and rebuilt at Deptford in 1715 with new carved work worth £28.17.0.

James Dickerson, Plymouth. (78,79) After a joint entry with Samuel Dickerson in 1790 James Dickerson went on to work on his own, probably in 1794 when he advertised: "Wanted an apprentice to a Ship Carver. Apply to James Dickerson, Master Carver, Plymouth Yard." One of his earliest contracts was carved work for two 2nd rates of 80 guns, *Caesar* launched in 1793 and *Gibraltar,* the Spanish *Fenix* captured in 1780, for which he was paid £44.8.0. A more lucrative proposition was *Plymouth Yacht* built in 1796 for which he received £96.7.6. In 1801 he cut carved work for three French prizes, 3rd. rates captured in 1798, *Hercule,* 74 guns, *Donegal,* ex *Hoche,* 76 guns, both of which received new heads for £25 and new quarters for £20. The other, *Canopus* ex *Franklin* of 80 guns had her "figurehead wounded by shot and rendered totally unserviceable" and this was replaced for £33. Even prison ships had to have their appearance maintained and in 1807 *Bedford* ex 3rd. rate of 74 guns was refurbished. Dickerson also cut carved work for the yard at Milford Haven (sometimes called Pembroke), among them *Milford* another 74 gun 3rd. rate which brought in £21. More French prizes were brought in for him to overhaul, nine between 1807 and 1811. Two of his most important contracts were the 120 gun 1st. rates *Caledonia* of 1808 and *Nelson* launched in 1815 with bust figureheads that cost £35 each.

James Dickerson was still carver in Plymouth as late as 1828. He had started to carve a full length figure for *Royal Adelaide,* a 104 gun 1st. rate, launched in 1828 after being on the stocks for nine years, when the Admiralty changed its mind and ordered a bust. Dickerson demanded payment for the work done on the first head, estimated at £15. The Admiralty must have changed their minds again as a full length standing figure of *Royal Adelaide* stood outside Chatham Dockyard for many years.

Samuel Dickerson, Plymouth. The reduced entries in the Admiralty ledgers show that between 1770 and 1790 Samuel Dickerson only earned between £88 and £170 a year from his work. This is odd because, at the time, he was described as "the famous dockyard sculptor who was employed at Plymouth". When he prepared his quotation for the decorative work for *Narcissus* of 1781, 6th. rate 21 guns he described his proposed design thus:-"In the middle of the taffrail is a figure of Narcissus, in a reclining attitude, admiring himself in a brook. He is attended by two young Pans, diverting himself with their musical reeds, and radiant in a garlands of flowers. On the larboard of the taffrail is a rabbit as being native of the woods, and on the starboard a dog is depicted by way of contrast, trees, flowers, plants and shrubs are introduced to complete the picture .On the larboard quarter-piece is a figure of Diana standing on a pedestal, and on the corresponding starboard quarter-piece is the figure of Echo clothed in light drapery, the whole design being completed with an introduction of contrasts." Some of his sketches were still in existence in 1900 but have since vanished. While he was carver a number of ' ships of the line' were launched at Plymouth, 3rd. rate of 74 guns such as *Conqueror* of 1773, 3rd. rate of 64 guns like *Monmouth* of 1772, and *Royal Sovereign* a 1st. rate of 100 guns in 1786. His name appears between 1787 and 1790 jointly with that of James Dickerson.

Frederick Dickerson, Plymouth. (81). From 1832, when he was 24 years old, until 1860, the name Frederick Dickerson appears in letters between the Admiralty and the dockyard at Plymouth. During this period he carved figureheads for at least 30 warships and several of these have survived to this day. The Admiralty was always keeping an eye on costs and provided the Superintendent of the dockyard at Plymouth with prices of carved work supplied by the carvers in London in order that he might keep a check on Dickerson's prices for equivalent figureheads. Among the more important figureheads which he executed were *Royal William* (81), built at Pembroke Dock in 1833, a 1st. rate 120 guns, *St. George*, built at Plymouth in 1840, a 1st. rate 120 guns, for both of which he carved new figureheads in 1859 costing £35 each, and *Albion* built at Plymouth in 1842, a 2nd. rate 90 guns £35. Small figureheads came cheaper at £6 for *Peterel* of 1860, a wooden screw sloop, and *Inflexible*, of 1845, a wooden paddle sloop. In the 1851 census he described himself as an "artist and naval carver, aged 43."

Alexander Pettigrew Elder, London. Elder was born in Dundee in 1828 and first appears in the London directories in 1853 in Limehouse. He tried to get himself on to the Admiralty list of approved carvers, but met with little success. In 1856 he sent a sketch for a figurehead for *Victoria* a 1st. rate of' 121 guns, a screw warship, and although he carved a model for this, he was not successful in his bid. However, in 1857 he was authorised to carve a figurehead for *Charybdis* (84), a wooden screw corvette of 2,187 tons and this was the only order which he received from the Navy. In 1859 this figurehead was examined but "officers did not consider that it was in any way superior to those usually furnished."

George Faldo, London. In a letter which he wrote in 1832, Faldo mentions that he had been in the ship carving business for 24 years and his family also, before he was born. There is no evidence whether or not George Faldo carved for the Navy before he went into partnership with Richard Overton in 1824 to form Overton & Faldo, an association which only lasted until 1829. In his letter he recalled that he had cut the figurehead for *Thunderer*, a 2nd. rate 84 guns, launched in 1831 and had provided the carved work for *Vernon* of 1832, a 4th. rate 40 guns. Here he seems to have run into trouble. He had carved a full length figurehead which had not met with approval after the Navy had seen it fitted on the ship and he offered to carve out the legs to form scrolls and drapery. There is no indication that this was ever done but the replacement, which was carved in 1846 by the Hellyers, was certainly only a half length figure and this has been preserved in Portsmouth. Faldo was very unhappy that another carver's quotation had been accepted in preference to his own and he issued a warning that this had happened before and that the customer had always come back to him having been disappointed. Faldo must have offended the Admiralty with the tone of his letter as he did not receive another order and the only other letters from him are an offer to carry out work on *Firebrand*, a screw steamer for £24.12.8. in 1833 and much later in 1854 when George Faldo and Sons forwarded designs for a figurehead for the *Viper*.

84. Virago, *(a bold woman), carried this figurehead carved by a Hellyer. She was a wooden paddle sloop of 1,059 tons b.m., built in Chatham in 1842. Small compared with other carvings she is attractively wrought.*

84. Charybdis *was a wood screw corvette of 2,187 tons built in Chatham in 1859 and carried the only figurehead carved by A. P. Elder for the Navy. While preserved at Rosyth she was called "the lady in the black nightie" by the small daughter of the Commanding Officer.*

Thomas Fletcher, Chatham. (90).   The Fletchers seem to have been an accomplished family and no fewer than three of them carved for the Navy during the 17th. century. Thomas Fletcher was the first to be named in the Accountant General's ledgers. Most of his early work seems to have been repairs as the sums of money involved were nowhere near the cost of decorating a new warship. However with the return to the throne of Charles II a number of vessels were renamed and their carved work was altered or replaced. *Sovereign of the Seas* of 100 guns was rebuilt in 1660 and Fletcher received £109. *Taunton* of 1654 of 48 guns was renamed *Crowne* in 1660 bringing in £87.10.0 followed by *Royal Charles* ex *Naseby*, 80 guns which earned him £51.16.0. Britain was at war with the Dutch from 1664 to 1667 and 1672 to 1674 and battle damage had to be mended giving Fletcher a steady income. In 1679 Parliament authorised the construction of thirty warships and Thomas Fletcher received his share. *Britannia* of 1682, 1st. rate, 100 guns, cost £895.19.4, while further down the scale came *Pendennis* of 1679, a 3rd. rate 70 guns, which fetched in only £160.

The entry in the ledger for *Britannia* shows how carefully the Admiralty kept control on expenditure, requiring five officials to keep an eye on the carver:
"To Thomas Fletcher of Chatham, carver, the 12th. February 1682 for the price of the severall Carved Works by him performed on board His Majesty's Shipp *Britannia* between March 1679 and 20th. October 1682, the same being measured by Mr. Robert Lee, Mr. John Shish, Mr. Josiah Lawrence, Mr. Daniel Furzer and the Clerk of the Cheque and them according to their certificate on this Bill the sum of Eight Hundred and Ninety-five Pounds Nineteen Shillings and Fourpence.'

He was involved in a minor scandal in 1674 when the Master Shipwright was 'investigated' in connection with work done on his house using dockyard labour which included the services of the carver Thomas Fletcher.

Matthew (Matthias) Fletcher, Chatham, Deptford and Sheerness (82).   Matthew

Fletcher appears in 1679 when the first of the thirty new warships was being built. He seems to have shared the work on *Sandwich,* a 2nd. rate of 90 guns, as the £120.15.0 which he received does not represent the full cost for this class. This vessel had been built at Harwich and Fletcher received an extra £150 to cover expenses for himself and his workmen in travelling down to Harwich. Matthias Fletcher was another carver who benefited from the mis-management of naval affairs. When Samuel Pepys returned to the Admiralty in 1685 it was found that 85% of the fleet was unfit for service. He started slowly on a programme of overhaul and as his position became more secure he began to speed up the work. During the first six months of 1687 and early 1688 Fletcher worked on seventeen warships from the 42 gun *Bonaventure* of 1650 to the 54 gun *Greenwich* of 1666, being paid only £118.9.10 for his pains. In 1687 a new 4th. rate brought him £70.0.0. In 1687 he was paid for the work which he had carried out on *Albermarle,* a 2nd. rate, 90 guns, launched in 1680. He had worked alongside John Fletcher and they shared the payment of £404.10.0. *Albermarle* was back in his hands 15 years later for repairs at a cost of £38.0.0. Matthew Fletcher worked for various naval yards along the River Thames and was kept busy executing carved work for new warships:

Deptford	1693	*Torbay*	2nd. rate, 80 guns	£182.14.6
Sheerness	1693	*Medway*	4th. rate, 60 guns	£157.13.0
Chatham	1698	*Somersett*	3rd. rate, 80 guns	£257.19.0
Woolwich	1687		new 4th. rate	£70. 0.0

The War of the Spanish Succession began in 1702 bringing with it the usual upsurge in repairs. After the Battle of Vigo in October 1702 Fletcher worked on the 1st. rate, 100 gun *Royal Sovereign* of 1701, four 2nd. rates including *Association* of 1697, and a 3rd. rate. Joseph Wymhurst shared the work on these vessels. Between 20th. April 1702 and 5th. June 1703 Matthew Fletcher carried out repair work on 38 ships, from as little as 3/- for *Squirrel* yacht, 4 guns, built in 1694, to £8.10.0 for *Shrewsbury,* 2nd. rate, 80 guns, built in 1695. At this time a middleman seems to have become involved as, for a while, payments for carved work were not made direct to the carver but to a Richard Fremple and Jonathan Nunn. Matthew Fletcher worked alongside Thomas Davidson on *Vigo* 4th. rate, 48 guns, when she was refitting after her recapture in 1702. The 4th. rate, 60 gun *Kingston* of 1697 came to Chatham after the capture of Gibraltar in July 1704. Amongst his last contracts were two vessels launched in 1711, *Bonaventure,* a 4th. rate, 50 guns, building at Chatham and *Scarborough* a 5th. rate, 32 guns, building at Sheerness.

John Fletcher, Chatham and Deptford. The last of the Fletchers was John Fletcher who started working at Chatham shortly after Samuel Pepys had been appointed to the Admiralty. Pepys found the ships of the fleet in a state of neglect with 142 of them unfit to be sent into action. In 1687 Fletcher carried out repairs to the carved work of twenty-one vessels and presented a bill for £278.18.0, a modest sum by the standards of the day. In 1688 the ledger clerk began once more to name the ships for which the money was being paid out and included *Albermarle,* a 2nd. rate, 80 guns, built in 1680 on which £404.10. was spent, the work being shared with Matthias Fletcher. One of the ledgers gave even more detail, and in this case described the work done:
"To John Fletcher 14th. March 1688 for the carved work performed on board his Majesty's Shipps at Chatham. *Montague* (3rd. rate built in 1654 as *Lyme*), *Hampton Court* (3rd. rate, 70 guns, built in 1678).

Upper deck ports	19 @ 17/- ea	£16. 0.3
Quarter--do--	5 @ 12/-	3. 0.0
Taffrells, 10 ft. long, 2 ft. deep, 6½ in. thick	2 @ 55/- ea	5.10.0
Brackets, 3½ ft. long, 7 in, thick.	11 @ 9/- ea.	4.19.0
Peeces of Buttons for Topps of ye gallerys, 5 ft. long, 4 in. thick	9 @ 3/- ea	1. 7.0
Wing for ye support, 3 ft. long, 4 in. thick		9.0
A Lyon for ye Head, 15½ ft. long, 2 ft, thick		4.10.0
Brackets, 5 ft. long, 10 in. broad.	8 @ 14/- ea.	5.12.0

86. *This is Robert Hall's sketch of the figurehead for* Firefly, *a wooden paddle survey vessel of 360 tons b.m., launched at Woolwich in 1832. Fortunately he was a better carver than he was an artist. (Public Record Office ADM 87/3.)*

86. *Grayfoot & Overton sent this sketch to the Navy Board for* Tribune, *a 5th. rate of 36 guns, built in 1803 at Burlesden. Damage to her carved work necessitated a new figurehead in 1814. (Public Record Office ADM 106/1794.)*

A mask for ye catheads		7.0
Bulkhead brackets for ye Forecastle, 6 ft. long, 5 in. broad.	4 @ 11/- ea.	2. 4.0
Bracket for ye steerage, 8½ ft. long, 5 in. thick.	3 @12/- ea.	1.16.0
do-- for ye bulkhead, 6½ ft. long, 4 in. thick	3 @ 10/-	1.10.0
Belfry capp, 4½ ft. broad, 2 in. thick.		2 .5.0
Hansings, 4½ ft. long, 9 in. thick	2 @ 7/-	14.0
Knightheads	2 @ 5/-	10.0
Head brackets, 5 ft. long, 6½ in. broad,		12.0
--do-- 5½ ft. long, 8 in. thick		12.0
One whole port of four quarters 5½ ft. thick, 71 in. broad and 3 ft. diameter to ye outside of ye port.		1.10.0
Hawse piece in ye waist 3 ft. long, 6 in. broad.		8.0
Ports 5 ft. diameter, cut leaves and flowers	6 @ 18/- ea.	5. 8.0
Gallery brackets, 4½ ft. long, 8 in. broad.	6 @ 9/-	2.14.0
A supporter for ye cathead, 13 ft. long, 15 in. broad		2.10.0
Bulkhead bracket, 2 ft. long, 7 in. thick	3 @ 5/- ea.	1 .1.0
A dogg for ye hansings, 3½ ft. long.		1 .2.0
Knightheads	3 @ 5/- ea.	15.0
		£77 8.0 "

Once more the clerk started giving 'blanket' entries and in 1692 recorded the payment of £3,046.9.0.

Goddard, London.   When the 5th. rate 44 gun *Dover* was built in 1740 by Bronsden & Wells of Deptford a carver by the name of Goddard was paid £33.0.0 for cutting her carved work.

Grayfoot and Overton, London, (86),(101).   (The Admiralty correspondence was frequently addressed to Grayfoot & Co.). As far as is known John Grayfoot and Richard Overton originally worked on merchant ships, but in 1812 they completed carved work for *Indus,* a 3rd. rate 74 gun frigate built by the Dudman yard at Deptford. However this did not give them automatic acceptance by the Naval Yards and in 1816 they had to submit samples of their carving to Deptford. These were approved and they were put to work on the new yacht *Royal George.* Later in the year they were requested to provide prices for "standing figures with emblems" for various classes of warship. When the yard sent these to the Admiralty they added, for comparison, the prices which William Burrough had charged 25 years before:

Size of ship	Grayfoot & Overton.	W. Burrough
120/100 guns	£46. 0.0.	
98	£38. 0.0.	
80	£35. 0.0.	
74	£31.12.0.	£22. 0.0.
50	£22.16.0.	£14.16.0.
38/36	£17.10.0.	£11. 0.0.
32	£15. 0.0.	£ 9. 0.0.
24/20	£ 9.10.0.	£ 6.10.0.
sloop	£ 7.10.0.	£ 6.10.0.

When the work on *Royal George* was completed later in 1816 the Admiralty questioned the amount of the bill. Deptford explained that the time spent had been equivalent to one man working for 440 days, and taking 10/- per day as a fair wage and adding 25% for profit this would give a cost of £275. They therefore considered the carver's charge of £279.11.6 to be reasonable. In 1820 the two shipyard carvers, Whitfield and Keast, were overwhelmed with work and the Dockyard sought permission to bring in Mrs. Lucy Burrough and John Grayfoot to undertake the carving for *Russell*, a 3rd. rate 74 guns, built Deptford 1822, *Southampton* 4th. rate 60 guns, built Deptford 1820 and *Ariel*, a 10 gun brig sloop built Deptford 1820. In 1822 the 'in-house' carvers Whitfield and Keast were discharged by order of the Admiralty, leaving *Aeolus* 5th. rate of 46 guns (launched 1825) with a figurehead unfinished and *Algerine* a 10 gun brig sloop (launched 1823) with none. Grayfoot & Overton were engaged to complete the one figurehead and to carve others for ships approaching

87. *The figurehead for* Active, *a 5th. rate of 36 guns, built in Chatham in 1845 was carved by a Hellyer. She is beautifully executed and more lifelike in appearance than many naval carvings.*

87. *There is a family story that when the Duke of Wellington saw the figurehead which a Hellyer had carved for* Waterloo, *a 1st. rate of 120 guns, built in 1833, he was not happy about the size or shape of the nose. He was even less pleased when the carver told him that as far as he was concerned the nose was true to life.*
(Craig/Farr collection)

completion.

The last entry in the Trades Directory for Grayfoot & Overton is made in 1824 when the partnership changes. From 1825 the Admiralty engaged the services of Overton & Faldo.

Robert Hall, London.   Hall was one of the few carvers on the Admiralty's list during the 19th. century though the records show that the work he performed was generally for the smaller warship, *Cleopatra* of 1835, 6th. rate 26 guns, (81), *Firefly* of 1832, survey vessel, (86), *Star* of 1835, an 8 gun packet brig. He was given an order for a new figurehead for *Edinburgh*, 3rd. rate 74 guns of 1811, "the old being decayed", but this was countermanded as another carver had already been awarded the contract. Robert Hall was, however, given the order for cutting the carved work for *Vanguard*, 3rd. rate 78 guns of 1835 for £30, with faces for the catheads at 25/- each. In 1835 he was invited to tender for the new figurehead for *Howe*, a 1st. rate 120 gun ship built in 1815, but he was in competition with the Hellyer family and his bid was unsuccessful. The Navy was still as slow in paying bills as they had been a hundred years before. In 1834 Hall executed carved work for *Cleopatra* and *Carysfort*, 6th. rate 26 guns but had to wait until 1839 before he was paid for the work. During the five years that he worked for the Navy, Hall worked on about 38 ships, providing figureheads for 21 of them. He did not receive any more work after 1837 although several times he wrote to "solicit permission to quote for carved work." He may have offended the Admiralty when, in 1839, he declined to give an estimate for the carved work for *Royal Sovereign*, a 1st. rate 110 guns which was never built. In 1860 he wrote to the Admiralty once more, again unsuccessfully, though his request was given some consideration. Naval officers were instructed to inspect some of his work but they reported adversely, saying: "We do not consider from two figureheads carved by Mr. Hall for merchant ships that they are so artistic or well executed as those supplied for the Royal Navy."

Joseph Helby, Deptford and Woolwich.   In the late 1600s during the period of modernisation of the Navy, the extensive carved work which was required to decorate the warships of the period sometimes required the combined forces of two carvers. Joseph Helby executed the carved work of three warships in company with John Leadman:

Bill paid:

21st. May 1679	3rd. rate		Woolwich	£160
30th. July 1679	3rd. rate, 70 guns	*Stirling Castle*	Deptford	£160
30th. July 1679	3rd. rate			£160
Later he worked on his own:				
28th. Feb. 1694	2nd. rate, 80 guns	*Cambridge*	Deptford	£183 4. 9
31st. Dec. 1696	3rd. rate		Deptford	£160
7th. July 1697	2nd. rate, 80 guns	*Ranelagh*	Deptford	£189.14.3

Helby had a profitable business judging from the fact that during the eight months April to December 1695 he received from the Admiralty payments totalling £614.19.0. Unfortunately at this time the accounts clerk was not recording any detail against the payments. Later the books gave ships' names and reveal *Britannia*, a 1st. rate of 100 guns, built in 1701 as a 'one-off, no expense spared' contract with Helby receiving £1,623.16.4 for executing her carved work. In 1702-1703, as with some of the other carvers, Helby seems to have worked through another contractor Nathaniel Jackson, both for Deptford and Woolwich. At the time he was carrying out repair work, as well as carving for new vessels. *Swallow*, a 4th. rate 54 guns for which he received £84.6.0, and *Garland*, a 5th. rate 44 guns which brought him £49.19.0. Two of his last contracts were the rebuilding of *Isabella* of 1683, a yacht with 8 guns, rebuilt at Deptford in 1703 at a cost of £53.10.6 for carved work, and *Devonshire* of 1692, a 3rd. rate 80 guns which cost only slightly more at £61.5.0 in 1704. Helby was one of the carvers who was entrusted with the regular maintenance of the decorative carving aboard the Royal yachts. Between 1700 and 1706 he carried out repairs on *Fubbs* of 1682 and later he was paid £308.17.4 of which £292.0.2 was for a rebuild of the hull in 1707. *Katherine*

89. *This is the Hellyer's sketch for the figurehead of* Superb, *a 2nd. rate of 80 guns, built in 1842, portraying the young Queen Victoria, a very popular subject for naval figureheads. As well as being good carvers the Hellyers were also excellent artists. (Public Record Office. ADM 87/12.)*

89. *In complete contrast was the warrior figurehead for* Mars, *a 2nd. rate of 80 guns, another Hellyer design. She was built in 1848 and eventually became a training ship at Dundee. The figurehead was taken ashore but decayed. (Public Record Office, ADM 87/17.)*

cost the taxpayer £225.7.11 between 1705 and 1707.

One of the last vessels on which he worked had an eventful career. *Milford,* a 5th. rate of 32 guns was built as *Scarborough* in 1694, captured by the French in 1694, recaptured in 1696 and renamed *Milford.* She was rebuilt in 1705 and Helby was paid £139.16.0.

The Hellyer Family, London.(73, 84, 87, 89, 93, 95).   Although the Hellyer family were in the wood carving business from around 1500 it was only the later generations which carried out work for the Naval dockyards. Their name appears first on a quotation in 1803 for a new figurehead for *Phoenix,* a 5th. rate of 38 guns built in 1783. It was signed by William Mattingley followed by Edward Hellyer's name. Payments had been made to Mattingley & Co. since 1799 and it may be that Edward Hellyer was the "& Co." 1810 saw Hellyer signing quotations though it was still under the heading " Wm. M. & Co." but in 1811 he was signing offers as Edward Hellyer & Son starting with a new head for *Elephant,* a 74 gun 3rd. rate of 1786, £16, a price which was cut by the Navy Board to £11.

With the Napoleonic War in progress there was plenty of work and a continual procession of ships passed through their hands. *Furieux* a French 5th. rate of 38 guns captured in 1809, £6 for a new head. In 1812 £21 for a head for *Minden* a 74 gun 3rd. rate building in Bombay. *Bulwark* a 3rd. rate of 74 guns built in 1807 needed a new figurehead in 1813 costing £21. In 1816 they received approval of the design of a figurehead for *Princess Charlotte* a 1st. rate of 104 guns, but they were not permitted to proceed until 1824 by which time the Navy Board had cut the price to £46. In 1819 the elm wood figurehead of *Hyperion* a 5th. rate of 32 guns built in 1807 was found to be rotten and a new one was cut from American fir. Between 1811 and 1824 the Hellyers cut at least 18 figureheads for new vessels and 32 to replace damaged ones. One of the replacements was for *Defiance,* formerly a 74 gun 3rd. rate which was being converted into a prison ship!

Continuous records are available from 1830 to 1860 and during this period they were the

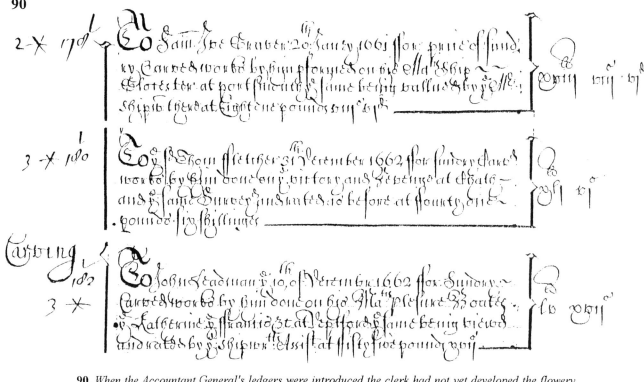

90. *When the Accountant General's ledgers were introduced the clerk had not yet developed the flowery style which is displayed in later years.(74, 80) nor had he begun to group the entries under names. The above brief statements read:*
"To Samuel Ive carver 20th. January 1661 ffor price of sundry carved work by him performed on His Majesty's ship Forester *at Portsmouth ye same being valued by ye Master Shipwright there at Eighteen pounds Eight Shillings and sixpence."*
" To Thomas Ffletcher 31st. December 1662 ffor sundry carved worke by him done on ye Victory *and* Revenge *at Chatham and same surveyed and valued as before at Fortyone pounds six shillings.*
" To John Leadman ye 10th. of December 1662 ffor sundry carved worke by him done on His Majesty's Pleasure Boats ye Katherine *and ye* Francis *at Deptford ye same being reviewed and rated by ye Shipwright's Assistant at ffiftyfive pounds seven shillings."*
One rather delightful feature of this ledger is, that having carefully entered all the costs in Roman numerals the clerk then entered the total in Arabic numerals.
(Forester, 22 guns, built 1657, Victory, 42 guns, built 1620, Revenge, 42 guns, purchased 1650, Katherine, 8 guns, built 1661 and Francis, 14 guns, captured 1657).
(Public Record Office ADM 20/4)

main carvers to the Navy cutting carved work for at least 234 vessels, including new warships from every naval dockyard. They probably carried out more than this but many of the letters refer to "the carver" without naming him. They executed figureheads for newly launched ships, new figureheads for those which had lost theirs due to decay or accident, and they carried out repairs to general decorative carving. Among the new figureheads were several for ships built at Bombay including *Madras* 2nd. rate, 80 guns, renamed *Meeanee* before she was launched in 1848. *Malacca* of 1853, 6th. rate 26 guns, *Zebra,* renamed *Jumna* before her launch in 1848, a 16 gun brig, and *Goshawk,* a 12 gun brig launched in 1847 and renamed *Nerbudda.* In 1840 they carved a figurehead for *Royal Frederick,* a 1st. rate of 110 guns, but before it could be fitted the vessel was renamed *Queen* and Hellyers were requested to make extensive alterations to the figurehead to suit the new name. In 1846 they were asked to make more changes but J. E. Hellyer pointed out that there was not much wood left to work on and what there was, was badly decayed. He wanted the Admiralty to authorise a new figure and even more he wished to be paid for the work that he had already carried out, viz: £21.12.0. Whether or not his request was granted is not clear, but *Queen* did get a new figurehead in 1858. In 1844 the Hellyers carved two figureheads for the wooden paddle sloop *Janus* at £5.10.0 each. This seemed odd, as, although Janus was the two-headed god who looked both ways, why buy two figureheads? An article in The Illustrated London News gave the answer. The *Janus* of 763 bm. was a double ended vessel with a sharp bow and a sharp stern, designed to operate in narrow creeks, fitted with a rudder at each end and a figurehead at each end.

They did not have the field to themselves, being in competition with Frederick Dickerson in

Plymouth and Robert Hall in London. George Faldo and Nehemiah Williams of London received occasional orders. In 1850 dominance of the Hellyers was challenged by Nehemiah Williams who submitted a schedule of prices which considerably undercut those of the Hellyers. To meet this the Hellyers reluctantly dropped their prices but warned of a drop in quality, a fact which did not seem to worry the Admiralty. Providing a figurehead for the Admiralty could be a protracted business. In December 1851 the Hellyers quoted £20 to carve a figurehead for *Imperieuse* a wooden screw frigate of 2,358 b.m. (launched in 1852). In May 1855 they had not received authority to proceed, but they assured the Admiralty that once they received an order they could complete the work in two weeks. A year later Deptford advised them that the mould for the block for the figurehead was ready in their mould loft, but they had no yellow pine in stock wherewith to make the block. They had asked Woolwich to help out but that yard had also run out. The next mention of *Imperieuse* was in 1858 when Hellyers presented their bill for payment.

The most famous figurehead carved by the Hellyer family was that of *Warrior*, the first 'ironclad', a huge figure which weighed about 2½ tons. The original carved in 1860 represented a Saracen with a scimitar, but when this was lost in an accident in 1872 it was replaced by another figure from a Hellyer chisel, this time more in a Roman style with a short stabbing sword. Although *Warrior* herself has survived to this day the figurehead was allowed to decay and a new one has had to be carved by Jack Whitehouse and Norman Gaiches on the Isle of Wight.

The Admiralty records after 1860 were severely pruned and only a few representative volumes were kept. From these we find that the Hellyers were still carving naval figureheads in 1876, among them the iron screw corvette *Bacchante* of 4,130 tons, built in Portsmouth, and that they were providing carved work for the Thames-side builders R. & H. Green. In 1885 Palmers Ironworks, shipbuilders on the Tyne, launched the despatch steamer *Surprise,* 1,650 tons, with "carved work by Hellyer of London and Shields." In 1888 the ironclad *Victoria,* 10,470 tons, was towed down the Tyne " bearing an extravagant emblem on her bow, the work of Hellyer Bros." She was a product of the Armstrong, Mitchell shipyard. The family were kept busy for many months on the carved work for the German battleship *Kaiser Wilhelm* built by the Thames Ironworks.

Abraham (Ambrose) Hunt, Kinsale Over the period February 1696 to March 1703 a carver by the name of Abraham or Ambrose Hunt carried out repair work on warships at Kinsale. Of the first three for which he cut carved work for £27.0.10, one, *Hastings* a 5th. rate of 32 guns built in 1695 was wrecked in 1697. Other vessels on which he worked were the 5th. rate 32 gun *Rye,* of 1696, £3.8.6. and *Feversham,* 5th. rate, 32 guns, of 1696, £6.2.6. The money was paid through an agent named Daniel Wiseman.

Samuel Ive. (sometimes spelled Ivie or Ivey) (90). Samuel Ive worked for a short time at Portsmouth. He started when Charles came back to England in 1660 and much of his work would have been altering or adding decoration to vessels built during the Commonwealth. Among the vessels on which he worked were *Foresight,* of 50 guns built 1650 and *St. Andrew,* a 42 gun ship of 1622 which brought him in £92.16.6, and *Monk,* 60 guns of 1659, £25.0.0. The payments which were relatively small for the period included *Milford,* 22 guns of 1654 and *Phoenix,* 38 guns of 1647 for which he was paid £66.2.0. Ive died in 1667.

Robert Jones. Starting in 1710 Robert Jones spent about eleven years working for the dockyard at Woolwich. His contracts in 1711 included three new vessels, *Hind,* a 6th. rate 20 guns, *Blandford,* a 6th. rate 20 guns and *Ormonde,* a 4th. rate 54 guns, bringing in a total of £38.4.6. He executed decorative carving on *Royal George* a 1st. rate of 100 guns, built in 1673 as *Royal Charles* and rebuilt and renamed *Royal George* in 1715 for which he received £130.0.0. The rest of the time he was busy with repair work each contract worth only a small sum, varying from *Basilisk* of 1695, bomb, 2/9, to *Crowne,* built as *Taunton* in 1654, 48 guns, £12.19.0. One of his last jobs was re-decorating the rebuilt *Northumberland* in 1721, a 3rd. rate 70 gun ship which had been launched in

1705. Another major warship on which Jones executed carved work was a 1st. rate of 100 guns called *Britannia*, built in Woolwich in 1719 for which he was paid £220.5.0. At this point the accounts clerk decided to put in some detail.

" To carving the Taffrail with the King in the middle and several other   £53.10.0
figures, shields, trophies, ornaments etc.
For carving two quarter pieces, thwartships carved with the King's Armes,
Roses and Thistles, the Figures of Fame, Navigation and Mars with other
figures and ornaments.   61.10.0.
For carving the trailboards with Tritons sounding with shell Trumpets, Flaggs
and other ornaments.   7.10.0.

Nathaniel Keast, Deptford.   On May 31st, 1797 in response to an appeal from the various Master Carvers at the dockyards Nathaniel Keast, aged 43 was entered on the paybooks of the Deptford Dockyard along with George Whitfield. These two men were to be employed at 2/6 per day with no provision for extra earnings, working a six day week. In 1805 Whitfield and Keast became discontented with this arrangement as commercial wages for a carver outside the yard were higher and so they applied to the Dockyard officers for a rise in their wages. The officials were sympathetic and prepared a list of the work which the two men had carried out over a five month period, June to December 1804. To this list they applied the commercial carvers' rates and calculated that the men should be earning 4/11 per day. Surprisingly the Admiralty agreed that this would be the new rate. The list of work showed that they had executed carved work as follows:

Melampus	5th. rate 36 guns, built Bristol 1785. Sundry repairs.	£4.16.0.
Latona	5th. rate 38 guns, Built Limehouse 1781. Putting new arms on the figurehead and repairing its face. Various repairs.	4.19.0.
Drake	16 gun sloop. Purchased 1804. New wing for the figurehead	18/-
Hebe	5th. rate of 32 guns. Built in fir at Deptford 1804. A new figurehead for £7.6.0 and other repairs, totalling	23.10.0.
Royal Sovereign	yacht, built at Deptford 1804. A new figurehead representing His Majesty in Roman clothing with a scroll and with foliage for the knee.	8. 0.0.
	Other carving.	11.15.0.
Charlotte	yacht of 1749. Thirteen items of details in carved work.	9. 9.6.
Treasury Barge	Twenty-one minor items for repair.	48.11.6.

Note: Each man worked for 79 days.

The names of these men were removed from the paybooks in 1815 but they were kept on as carvers. A letter of 1820 refers to them as "the two carvers belonging to the yard" who were fully employed on *Venus,* a new 5th. rate of 46 guns and *Royal Sovereign*, a yacht of 1804. Other ships were on the stocks and the yard applied for permission to bring in Mrs. Lucy Burrough and John Grayfoot from outside to execute their carved work. The ships in question were *Russell* a 3rd. rate of 74 guns, completed at Deptford in 1822 after being 8 years on the stocks, *Ariel* a 10 gun brig sloop and *Southampton* a 4th. rate of 60 guns, both completed in Deptford in 1820. In 1822 the Admiralty was in the middle of an economy drive and instructed the yard to dismiss Whitfield and Keast. The yard obeyed but protested that *Aeolus* a 5th. rate of 46 guns was on the stocks with her figurehead half finished while *Algerine* a brig sloop of 10 guns had none. They then had to apply for permission to bring in Grayfoot & Overton to complete their requirements. To this the Admiralty agreed and these carvers completed the two ships in 1825 and 1823 respectively.

Richard Lawrence.   In 1778 a bill was submitted by Richard Lawrence for £31.12.8. The account did not indicate at which dockyard he worked.

John Leadman, Woolwich and Deptford. (90).   John Leadman was one of the leading carvers for the Navy in the 17th. century, and he worked at the yards at Woolwich and Deptford.

He, along with other carvers, seems to have benefited from the Restoration in 1660, as, for the next two years a succession of vessels passed through their hands for attention to their carved work. Some of the contracts were quite remunerative. In 1660 he worked on *Plymouth*, 60 guns of 1653, *Anne*, 58 guns of 1654, ex-*Bridgewater* and *Royal James*, 70 guns 3rd. rate, of 1658, newly renamed from *Richard*, for which he was paid a total of £100.13.8. Two other contracts paid equally well. *Kentish*, 46 guns of 1652, renamed *Kent*, £75.16.0. and *Preston*, 40 guns of 1653, renamed *Antelope*, £87.10.0. In 1667 he worked on *Royal Charles* ex *Naseby*, 80 guns built in 1655 and was paid £200.0.0. Only six years before Thomas Fletcher had received £51.16.0. for carving on the same vessel. The money was wasted as the Dutch took her as a prize later in 1667. In 1667 the 96 gun *London* caught fire and during the re-building of the hull Leadman had to provide new carved work to the value of £412.1.0. Leadman cut carved work for several new warships. At Deptford in 1666, *Cambridge*, a 3rd. rate, 70 guns which was billed at £90.0.0, and at Woolwich in the same year *Falcon*, a 5th. rate, 36 guns, which fetched Leadman £40.0.0. Also from Woolwich, in 1670, came *St. Andrew*, a 1st. rate 96 guns which cost £378.0.0.

He was another of the carvers who benefited from the order to build thirty new warships.

9th. June 1679	2nd. rate, 90 guns	*Windsor Castle*	Woolwich	£416
9th. June 1679	2nd rate, 90 guns	*Duchess*	Deptford	£416
9th. July 1679	3rd. rate, 70 guns	*Stirling Castle*	Deptford	£160
30th. July 1679	3rd. rate, 70 guns	*Hampton Court*	Deptford	£160

On the *Stirling Castle* he shared the work with Joseph Helby. He was probably the contractor for the 3rd. rate, 70 guns, *Burford*, *Captain*, and *Grafton*, also built in 1679 and each worth £160, and for the 2nd. rate 90 guns *Neptune*, built in 1683 which cost £423.13.4.

He carved the decorative work for at least one of the royal yachts, *Henrietta* of 1663, with 8 guns, at a cost of only £155.16.0. She passed through his hands again in 1672 when £105.0.0. was spent on smartening her up.

Cornelius Luck, London   Cornelius Luck placed entries in the Post Office Directories from 1861 to 1888. Two references to his work have been found, both for Admiralty contracts. He carved the figurehead for *Resistance* (96), an armoured frigate of 6,070 tons, built by Westwood & Baillie in 1861 for which he received £22.18.0, and until recently this outstanding figure could be

93. This was the proposal put forward by Overton & Faldo for Tyne, *a 28 gun 6th. rate, to be built in 1826. It represents Neptune and the vase with water pouring out was a device used by carvers when the name was a river or sea. (Public Record Office ADM 106/1800)*

93. We failed to find a Devil among the mercantile figureheads. This sketch shows a figurehead proposed by the Hellyers for the wooden paddle sloop Beelzebub *of 1,190 tons b.m. built in 1842. The vessel was in fact launched as* Firebrand. *(Public Record Office ADM 87/12)*

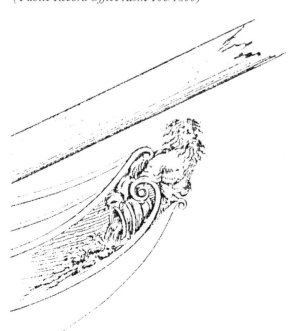

seen in the R. N. V. R. training centre in Glasgow. In 1877 he carried out the carved work for the screw corvettes *Garnet* and *Cormorant*, 1,130 tons, built at Chatham.

Cuthbert Mattingly, Plymouth and Portsmouth   The name Mattingly appears in the naval ledgers over a period of 23 years from 1737 executing carved work for the yard at Plymouth and 47 years from 1760 at Portsmouth. Most of the work was remedial with the occasional reconstruction. Many fetched as little as 3/- to £1.10.0. but *Canterbury*, 4th. rate, 60 guns of 1693 cost the navy £23.5.0. Rebuilding was more rewarding. *St. Albans* of 1706, 4th rate 54 guns, was rebuilt in 1737 and cost £47.17.5, *Kingston* of 1697, 4th. rate, 60 guns rebuilt 1740, £17.10.0. *Romney* of 1708, 4th. rate 54 guns reduced to 44 guns in 1745, £34.15.11. Two of the warships which took part in the surprise attack on Porto Bello in November 1739 received the ministrations of Cuthbert Mattingly, *Strafford* and *Worcester*, both 4th. rates, both built in 1735. The accounts clerk occasionally added some detail and from the invoices for 1742 to 1743 we find confirmation that the lion figurehead was commonly used.

Plymouth	4th. rate, 60 guns	1708	£17.10.0	a Lyon for the Head.
Sapphire	5th. rate, 44 guns	1740	10. 2.0	a Lyon for the Head.
Superbe	4th. rate, 60 guns	1736	17.10.0	a Lyon for the Head.
Jersey	4th. rate, 60 guns	1736	17.10.0.	a new Lyon for the Head
Chichester	2nd. rate, 80 guns	1695	1.18.0.	two legs and several locks for the Lyon.
Nonsuch	4th. rate, 50 guns	1741	14.0.	a piece for the Lyon 4 ft. 4 ins. long.

Over a period June 1746 to December 1747 nearly 50 vessels passed through his hands. Occasionally there was a newly built ship for which he would provide carved work. One of them was *Unicorn*, 6th. rate, 28 guns of 1748, £28.3.8. *Unicorn* was one of the first of a new breed of fast manoeuvrable frigates for the Navy with a design based on a captured French privateer called *Tigre*.

In 1755 the ledger clerk detailed the work for which payment was being made and the following gives some idea of the carvings with which warships of the period were adorned.
Dorset, yacht, 10 guns. built in 1753:-

Two new figures representing Africa and America for the stern @ £1.15.0. ea.	£3.10.0
Two festoons of flowers for the larboard badge	9.0
One piece of rail for the mizzen channel, 4 ft. long	4.0
Three pieces of frieze for the catheads	18.0
Twenty-six small pieces of the Taffrail, Quarter pieces, Frieze etc. @ 1/8 ea.	2. 3.4
Work done on board in several parts where defaced	14.0
The fore beam of the Awning carved 18 ft. long, @ 9d.per foot	13.6
Two sides of a ladder cut on each side	11.0

In 1755 *Warwick* of 1733, a 4th. rate 60 guns needed a complete new figurehead and was fitted with "a Lyon for the Head with fore leggs cut through", at the full allowable price of £17.10.0. Again money wasted as she was captured by the French shortly afterwards in March 1756. In about 1760 Mattingly moved to Portsmouth and was there until at least 1780 when the ledgers stopped entering the name of the yard, though he probably remained there until the entries ceased in 1807. During his first six months in Portsmouth he worked on 40 vessels including *Union*, a 2nd. rate of 90 guns, built in Chatham in 1756 for which he was paid £55.10.6, *Isis*, a 4th. rate of 50 guns, captured from the French in 1747 as *Diamant*, £26.14.6, and *Prince*, a 2nd. rate of 90 guns, built as *Triumph* in 1698, £45.0.0. For the remainder the highest payment was a mere £12.0.0. Later in 1760 Mattingly worked on three vessels captured in 1759 from the French at Lagos. *Modeste*, a 3rd. rate, 60 gun, £26.15.0, *Temeraire*, a 3rd. rate, 74 gun, £18.0.0, and *Blonde*, a 5th. rate, 32 gun, £15.17.1. From this time on the account books do not give ships' names, only total payments.

In 1773 Mattingley brought his son William into the business and in 1778 another carver named Jones was taken on to form Mattingley, Son, & Jones. In late 1780's Cuthbert Mattingley handed over the reins to his son and Mattingley & Jones were the carvers to the Portsmouth yard. Another change was made in the mid 1790's when Jones departed and Mattingley & Co. was formed, the "& Co." probably being Edward Hellyer whose name later began to appear on quotations below William Mattingley's signature. In 1803 they were offering to cut figureheads for *Phoenix* a 5th. rate of 38 guns built in 1783, a new head for £8, and *Princess Royal* a 2nd. rate of 90 guns built in 1773, a new head for £25. The documents were signed jointly until 1806 with Hellyer's name sometimes below "Wm. M. & Co." but after this year only Hellyer's name appeared on quotations. In 1810, a new partnership, Hellyer & Son, offered to cut the replacement figurehead for *Tweed* an 18 gun sloop built in 1807 to replace the one which had recently been carried away.

John Morley, Chatham and Sheerness. Shortage of work for ship carvers at the naval dockyards in 1797 led to carvers being laid off. The only employment available was that of labourer. On 7th. January 1797 John Morley late journeyman carver at Chatham and Sheerness petitioned the Admiralty to take him on to the yard paybooks as a labourer.

Maynard Nicholls, Plymouth. For eighteen months, between 1735 and 1736, Maynard Nicholls worked on three warships at Plymouth. Two of them were new 4th. rates of 60 guns, *Jersey,* for which he was paid £16.10.0 and *Weymouth* for which he received £37.10.0, his contribution to their carved work being a small one.

Overton & Faldo, Pageants, Rotherhithe. (101). (Frequently addressed as Overton & Co. in Admiralty letters). In 1825 Richard Overton took George Faldo as a partner in place of John Grayfoot. One of their first contracts was another of the frequent overhauls of the carved work on a royal yacht, in this case *Royal Sovereign* built in Deptford in 1804 for which they were to be allowed 8/- per day. They seemed to be taking rather a long time over the contract and to cover themselves the Deptford officers wrote to the Admiralty stating that they were worried about the delay in

95. *Admiral Lord Nelson was a favourite subject for naval figureheads and this imposing carving was executed by Hellyer & Browning for* Trafalgar, *a 1st. rate of 110 guns, built at Woolwich in 1841.*

95. Resistance *an armoured frigate of 6,070 tons was launched by Westwood & Baillie in 1861. The figurehead by Cornelius Luck was superbly carved in classical style, resembling a Greek statue. It was preserved in Glasgow, polished dark brown.*

completing the work but two men and an apprentice were employed on the job and they emphasised that despite their best efforts Overton & Faldo had been unable to find a competent ship carver in the district to assist them. In 1825 they were given the contract for carved work for *African*. This vessel was laid down in 1824 at Woolwich as a 10 gun sloop but was finally launched in 1825 as a wooden paddle steam tug. Despite her lowly status she had the full complement of carved work.

A bust head of an African	£4. 0.0.
A pair of cat faces	1. 4.0.
Two quarter pieces with full figures	7.10.0.
A bust of an African in the centre of the stern	£.3.10.0.
Carved elm board foliage on either side of same	3. 0.0.
Rich ornamental coves	3. 0.0.
Trusses and caps	15/- each.
Festoons	5/- each.
Two upper finishings and two lower finishings	6. 0.0.
Two cantilever brackets	1. 0.0.

This was followed in 1826 by an order for a more important vessel, *Barham*, a 3rd. rate of 74 guns built in Blackwall in 1811 and reduced to 50 guns in 1826 in Woolwich Dockyard, with a bust of a Senator in appropriate robes at £ 14.14.0, and for a new vessel building at Woolwich, *Tyne*, a 6th. rate of 28 guns, a bust of Neptune with emblems on the trailboards for £9.9.0. The Admiralty curtly deleted the decoration on the trailboards and reduced the price to £6. Frequently when the name of the vessel was that of a river or sea, the carver would incorporate a vase or jar from which water was being poured. The figure usually had little to do with water (93).

The partnership broke up in 1829.

Kingston Pavey, Plymouth.   In May 1797 the Master Carvers at the Naval Dockyards petitioned the Admiralty to take on to their books ship carvers who had been laid off due to lack of orders for decorative carvings on the warships. At Plymouth William Dickerson and Kingston Pavey were the two who were entered on the Yard Paybooks for the period 1797 to 1815 .They were to be paid the bare rate of 2/6 per day with no opportunity of earning more. The odd thing about the entries in the paybooks which recorded how much each man received was that the entry frequently read, "no payment, lent to the contractor." It is certain that the said contractor was in fact James Dickerson who was being paid direct from the Admiralty during this period.

Thomas Pierce, (Pearce), Plymouth.   Pierce began carving for the Plymouth yard in about 1753 and with the outbreak of the Seven Years War in 1756 he was kept busy with repairs to ships which were at sea in all weathers. Between June 1757 and June 1758 he worked on fortyone ships, mostly for small amounts, but among the more expensive repairs were *America*, a 5th. rate, 44 guns, built in 1757, which cost £15.8.6 and *Lyon*, a 3rd. rate, 60 guns, of 1701, £43.14.0. The French *Duc d' Acquitaine*, a 3rd. rate 44 guns, captured in 1757 was refurbished for £15.9.6 and a new 5th. rate, 36 guns *Brilliant* was decorated at a cost of £36.15.6 in 1757. In 1759 the Royal Navy won a resounding victory at Quiberon Bay and afterwards twelve of the warships involved came into Plymouth to receive attention from Thomas Pierce. Most of the bills were small but the captured French privateer *St. Florentine*, a 4th. rate of 60 guns needed £40.15.7. spent on her to bring her up to standard. One of his last new-building contracts was *Hero*, built in 1759, a 3rd. rate 74 gun frigate which brought him £95.12.0.

From this point the entries in the ledgers give no detail but the last recorded account was submitted in 1770 by Ann Pierce, presumably the widow of Thomas Pierce.

John Pippin, Plymouth.   In 1691 John Pippin was paid the sum of £4.6.0 for "carving a Lyon and delivering it into the Naval dockyard at Plymouth."

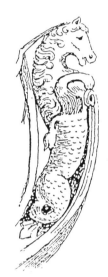

97. *(Top Right). The second class cruiser* Iris *was built in 1877 complete with clipper bow and a figurehead carved by Henry Trevenen of Plymouth.* (Munsey's Magazine.)
97. *(Right).* Seahorse *was a 6th. rate of 20 guns built in Portsmouth in 1712 when Robert Smith was Master Carver. Nelson served in her as a midshipman.*
(The Strand Magazine.)

97. *(Above). When* Black Prince, *an armoured frigate of 9,210 tons was built in Glasgow by R. Napier in 1861, the local carvers Kay & Reid were commissioned to cut this warlike image of the Royal Knight. (The Navy and Army Illustrated.)*

Thomas Pritchard. A payment to Thomas Pritchard of £44.7.3 was made in 1815 but no indication was given as to the yard in which he worked.

Phillip Reed, (Read), Plymouth. In the Archives in Exeter is a sacrament certificate dated 1714 for one Phillip Reed, carver at His Majesty's yard at Hamaoze (i.e. Plymouth). He began working there at the end of 1701, and in the following year the War of the Spanish Succession broke out and he was kept busy on a succession of repairs on damaged carved work, at one time 24 vessels in nine months. The most costly one was *Hastings* of 1698, a 5th. rate of 32 guns, which had £10.11.6 spent on her. During the early years of the war, the capture of Gibraltar in July 1704 was followed by a skirmish off Malaga in August. Afterwards four of the ships involved called at Plymouth including the 5th. rate 34 gun *Bedford* of 1698 which had been present at all three and cost £4.10.0 to repair. Ships were also being rebuilt and as this meant that all the planking was stripped from the upperworks, almost the whole of the carved work had to be replaced. The 66 gun *Rupert* was built in 1666 and rebuilt in 1703, being redecorated for £33.1.0. In addition new ships were being built and the 4th. rate, 50 gun *Strafford* of 1706 cost £35.4.0, while another, *Bristol*, a 4th. rate of 54 guns had carved work valued at £29.4.0 when she was launched in 1711.

In 1721 the accounts clerk decided to embellish his entries with a bit of detail and against the 3rd. rate, 64 gun *Ripon* of 1712 recorded:

A Trailboard   £1.10.0.
A quarter piece   12. 0.0.
Repairing the Lyon   4.10.0.

One of his last contracts was quite a large one, undertaken when *Norfolk* was rebuilt in 1728 with new carved work costing £96.0.0. She was a 3rd. rate of 80 guns which had been built in 1693. The Navy Office was not good at settling bills promptly and this bill was not settled until 1731. He had to wait until 1730 for payment for work which he executed in 1727 on *Experiment,* 5th. rate 32 guns built in 1689, a sum of £26.0.0, and *Drake,* a 2 gun yacht of 1705 for which he charged £24.14.0.

Robert Reynolds, Portsmouth.   In 1668 payments were made to Robert Reynolds of Portsmouth amounting to £107.14.0. This covered work on *Sovereign* of 100 guns built in 1637, and rebuilt in 1660, and other vessels which were not named. Only one other entry is detailed and covers work carried out in 1669 on *Resolution,* 3rd. rate, 70 guns, of 1667, *Mary,* 8 gun yacht of 1660, and *Bristol* 48 gun ship of 1653, £11.16.0 in all.

William Savage, Chatham and Sheerness.   When *Victory,* a 1st. rate 100 guns was launched in May 1765, she was fitted with one of the last figureheads which consisted of a group of figures. The specification which the carver was to follow ran to about 4,000 words, (about five of these pages), which described each item minutely, and it is one of the few specifications which has survived. Briefly *Victory's* figurehead consisted of a bust of the King in armour surrounded by four cherubs representing the four winds. On the starboard it was supported by a figure of Britannia and on the port side by a female figure representing Victory. This group was 24 ft. high, 18 ft. broad, and 12 ft. thick. Due to the extent of the decorative carving called for in the specification, three carvers were needed to execute the work and William Savage was brought in to assist Richard and Elizabeth Chichley between 1765 and 1766. In 1769 Savage was brought back to work with Elizabeth Chichley but after 1777 he was on his own. The last entry found was dated 1783.

By the time William Savage was appointed the entries in the ledgers had been reduced to figures only with no detail. However, during his tenure, among the vessels constructed at Sheerness were *Polyphemus,* a 3rd. rate, 64 guns, of 1782, *Bristol,* a 5th. rate, 50 guns, of 1775 and the 14 gun sloop *Fly* of 1776. At Chatham Savage would have provided the figurehead and decorative carving for *Alfred,* a 3rd. rate, 74 guns, of 1778, *Stirling Castle,* a 3rd. rate, 64 guns, of 1775 and *Amphion,* a 5th. rate, 32 guns, of 1780.

Unfortunately by now the entries in the ledgers contained no information about the vessels on which the carvers were working and gave only a date and the amount claimed. All too obvious is the time which elapsed between the presentation of the invoice and the payment. An account presented on the 29th. of April 1781 was not paid until the 31st. of October 1783. This two and a half year delay was quite common.

Lewis Sawyer, Portsmouth.   When the Admiralty authorised the construction of 30 new warships at the end of the 17th. century one of the carvers employed on the decorative work was Lewis Sawyer. The Accountant General's ledger for the period records one payment to him:
"To Lewis Sawyer 24th. Sept.1679 for the severall carved works performed by him on the new 3rd. rate lately building at Portsmouth, £150."

Robert Smith, Portsmouth. (97).   Robert Smith was engaged as carver to the Portsmouth yard from 1705 while the War of the Spanish Succession was under way. One of his first tasks was to cut the carved work for *Nassau,* a 3rd. rate, 70 gun vessel, launched in 1706, for £56.1.4. He carried out the usual remedial work, mainly small affairs except for *Lancaster* of 1694, a 2nd. rate, 80 guns, which had £57.10.0. spent on her in 1712. *Dolphin,* an 8 gun fireship of 1690 was rebuilt in 1711 and her cost was £20.3.0. 1712 saw the launch of *Success,* a 6th. rate of 20 guns whose decoration cost only £12.17.0. In 1719 Robert Smith was given a contract to cover the rebuilding of *Royal William.* She had been built in 1670 as *Prince* and renamed *Royal William* in 1692. Originally a 1st. rate of 100 guns she was rebuilt with 84 guns with new carved work costing £280.5.0. (In 1735 she was extensively redecorated by William Smith). Maintaining royal yachts was an expensive business and in 1721 Robert Smith was paid £71.13.9 for his work on the yacht *Dolphin,* of 1709. In 1722 *Lancaster* was back, this time to be rebuilt and to receive attention to her carved work to the tune of £41.3.0. The smaller *Captain* of 1678, 3rd. rate, 70 guns, cost the Navy £53.1.6 when she was rebuilt alongside *Lancaster*. One of his last contracts was *Kinsale*, a 5th. rate, 32 guns, built in 1700 and rebuilt in 1724 with redecoration costing £25.17.6.

William Smith, Portsmouth.   William Smith started in Portsmouth in 1724 during one of the rare periods of peace in English history. As a result he was engaged on repairing decayed carvings and those which had suffered storm damage. Mostly the amounts were quite small and in 1724 they ranged from 12/6 for *Blandford* of 1719, a 6th. rate, 20 guns, to £32.0.0. for *Ramillies* of 1664, a 2nd. rate, 82 gun ship. 1726 and 1727 saw an upsurge in the rebuilding of older warships, which necessitated the almost complete replacement of the carved work on the upper hull. Typical expenditures on redecorating work were *Aldborough,* a 6th. rate, 20 guns, of 1705, £17.17.0, *Adventure*, a 5th. rate, 40 guns, built in 1709, £21.8.0, the 4th. rate, 54 gun *Salisbury* of 1707, £22.10.0, while the 2nd. rate, 80 gun *Humber* of 1693 cost £51.10.0. One of William Smith's first big contracts was the carved work for an earlier *Victory*, a 1st. rate of 100 guns launched at Portsmouth in 1737. (She was lost by shipwreck in 1744.) For his efforts he was paid £142.12.0 which was slightly less than the permitted £166.12.0. The work which came his way included the occasional rebuild, such as *Princess Amelia,* a 2nd. rate, 80 guns, of 1693, rebuilt in 1728 with new carved work costing £31.14.0. *St. George*, a 1st. rate, 96 guns, was rebuilt in 1740 and the navy expended £147.8.0 on her carved work, a sum which represented an almost complete replacement of her decorative carving. She had been built in 1668 as *Charles* and renamed in 1687. In 1740 Britain was again at war in the War of the Austrian Succession and a steady flow of warships received attention at Portsmouth totalling 25 vessels in 12 months, ranging from *Royal William* (ex *Prince* of 1692), a 1st. rate, 100 guns, on which the Navy spent £28.16.0 down to the sloop *Grampus*, of 14 guns, built in 1731, which cost as little as £14.6.0. One of the new ships on which William Smith executed carved work was *Tilbury,* a 4th. rate, 58 guns, launched in 1745 for which he received the standard allowance of £65.7.2. *Milford,* a 4th. rate, 50 guns, of 1712 was rebuilt in 1744 and her refurbished carved work came to £47.11.5 which was again the standard figure.

One of William Smith's contracts which was recorded in full was the redecoration of the *Isis*, a 4th. rate, 50 guns, which had originally been the French *Diamant* captured in 1747:

"A head composed with the following work. In the front is a shield on which is cut the King of France's Coat of Arms with a crown intermixed with bands of reeds, scallop shells and other ornaments, on each side appears trophies of arms, Laurell, branches etc., richly adorned.	£13.2.0
Two pieces on the quarter gallery, on each piece is cut a shield with the King of France's cypher with grotesque work, double husks, scrolls, etc.	£4.10.0
For the taffrail in the middle is a Lyon's head, on each side are reeds with waving rafted leaves intermixed with grotesque work and variety of festoons of flowers, open double husks etc.	£16. 4.0
Two window lights cut with open grotesque work, scrolls, rafted leaves etc.	£1 12.0
Two brackets with rafted leaves	12.0
Repairing the walk in the stern, a piece in the centre cut with a sunflower	16.0
Four stiles between the lights cut with a variety of festoons of fruit and flowers	£1.10.0."

The detailed list also indicates that *Eagle*, a 3rd. rate, 64 guns, of 1745, *Ipswich,* a 3rd. rate, 70 guns, of 1694 and *Lyme,* a 6th. rate, 28 guns, of 1748 all had 'Lyon' figureheads. *Lyme* was a sister ship to the *Unicorn,* the first two true frigates which the Navy put into service, based on the captured French privateer *Tigre*. *Ferret* of 1743, a sloop of 14 guns, had on her bows the figure of Mercury which needed some small repairs. One of his last contracts was for the carved work for *Chichester*, a 3rd. rate, 70 guns, built in 1753. The cost of her carving was £87.16.0.

Henry Trevenen, Plymouth.   Henry Trevenen, carver and gilder of Plymouth was in the Trades Directory in 1856. The Admiralty records ceased in 1860 but in an isolated volume for 1876 there is some correspondence concerning the carved work for vessels built at Pembroke Dock which mention Trevenen's name relating to *Emerald* of 2,120 tons, launched 1876, a composite screw corvette, and another pair, launched later, *Iris* (97) in 1877, and *Mercury* in 1878, 2nd. class cruisers of 3,730 tons. One of the letters was correcting his design for *Mercury:* "The scroll should be held in the right hand."

Sebastian Vicars, Woolwich.   *Prince Royal,* a 64 gun ship built at Woolwich between 1608 and 1610 was elaborately decorated as was the custom of the period, at a total cost of £1,300. Sebastian Vicars was paid £441.0.4 for cutting the carved work.

Joseph Wade, Woolwich and Deptford.   In 1743 a small paragraph appeared in a London newspaper which read as follows: "On the same day died at Rotherhithe Mr. Wade, an eminent Ship Carver, esteemed to be one of the most ingenious men of his business." Joseph Wade had in fact been the master carver covering the Woolwich and Deptford yards. He was appointed in about 1716 in a time of peace and the work was mainly repairing damage to carved work, and replacing decorative carving affected by rebuilding work. Most of his early contracts were small but 1718 brought a spate of more paying work to Deptford. *Dursley Galley,* a 6th. rate, 20 guns, was built with decorative work valued at £31.10.0, while *Torbay,* a 2nd. rate of 80 guns built in 1693 was rebuilt with carved work costing £120.10.0. 1719 saw two new 6th. rate, 20 gun ships built at Deptford worth £36.14.0 each, *Greyhound* and *Blandford.* In about 1720 Wade was appointed Master Carver for Woolwich as well as Deptford. Two of the vessels for which Wade cut new carved work in 1725 were *Grafton,* a 3rd. rate, 70 gun ship, built in 1709, rebuilt at Woolwich with carving worth £78.5.0, and *Assistance,* a 50 gun ship, built in 1650, also rebuilt at Woolwich at a cost of £40.2.6. During the years before and after George II ascended to the throne in 1727 a number of the royal yachts were redecorated by Joseph Wade and expensively at that:

Fubbs	built. 1682	12 guns	1724	£370.12.11½
Mary	built. 1677	8 guns	1727	£286.11. 3½
William & Mary	built. 1694	10 guns	1738	£224. 4. 9½
Katherine	built. 1674	8 guns	1738	£264.17. 6½
Fubbs	built. 1682	12 guns	1738	£213 3 7½
Mary	built. 1677	8 guns	1742	£140 2 2½

Although the country was at peace the Navy undertook a programme of modernisation covering all rates and many of them passed through Wade's hands:

Prince George	built 1701	2nd. rate, 90 guns	1722	£137.15.0	(£300.0.0)
Antelope	built 1702	4th. rate, 54 guns	1741	47.11.5	(£ 47.4.5)
Squirrel	built 1707	6th. rate, 24 guns	1727	22.13.6	(£ 25.0.0)
Phoenix	built 1694	8 gun fireship	1727	22.13.6	
Northumberland	built 1705	3rd. rate, 70 guns	1742	87.16.2	(£ 87.16.2)

(She had already been rebuilt in 1721).
(The figures in brackets represent the sum allowed by the Admiralty for newly built ships).
     Wade also executed carved work for new warships:

Burford	built 1722	3rd. rate, 70 guns	Deptford	£89.16.0.
Captain	built 1743	3rd. rate, 70 guns	Woolwich	£87.16.2.

Even a humble store ship had to reflect the glory of the Navy and *Success* of 1709 was smartened up in 1727 for £27.4.6. (She was made a hulk in 1730.) Wade must have been delighted when in 1733 a decision was made to rebuild the yacht *Peregrine Galley* of 1700, a 6th. rate of 20 guns, and to rename her *Royal Caroline.* Wade was paid £1,358.18.7 for his work.
     Between 1727 and 1739 the entries in the ledgers read "Payment to Joseph Wade, senior and junior." Joseph Wade junior does not seem to have been appointed in his father's place,

Richard Walker, Deptford.   The name of Richard Walker appears only once when the

101. *This bust of* Queen Charlotte *was displayed on a wall in H.M.S. Excellent, the gunnery school at Portsmouth. She came from a 104 gun 1st. rate of that name, built at Deptford in 1810 when Whitfield and Keast were the carvers employed in the yard. It has been suggested that she had originally been fitted on a vessel of the same name, a 1st. rate of 100 guns built in Chatham in 1790 which blew up in 1800. Comparison with the head on the Dockyard model shows this to be very unlikely.*

101. *The Admiralty register records this figurehead as* Isis, *a 60 gun 4th. rate. She was laid down at Woolwich in 1813 as a 50 gun vessel, lengthened in 1816 to accommodate 60 guns and finally launched in 1819. The carvers Grayfoot and Overton do not seem to have had much knowledge of ancient legend as this armoured figure does not portray the Goddess of the moon.*

Admiralty paid him £400.4.8 for "sundry carved works by him performed on severall of His Majesty's shippes at Deptford between 1st. Jan. 1696 and 31st. March. 1696." Walker may not have been a carver as there are a large number of payments to him for painting ships at Deptford. He may have sub-contracted the carved work to a regular carver.

George Whitfield, Deptford (101). In 1797 ten ship carvers were laid off by the outside carving firms due to shortage of work at the five naval dockyards. The Admiralty were petitioned to give them employment and two were to be appointed to each of the five dockyards. At Deptford Nathaniel Keast, aged 43, and George Whitfield, aged 47, were entered on the yard paybooks. Even this did not guarantee them a steady income as in some years, George Whitfield received no payment from the Navy. This arrangement lasted until 1815 after which no carvers were kept in the Dockyard labour force. His activities are recorded under Nathaniel Keast.

George Williams, Chatham (81). George Williams started work as ship carver at the Naval Dockyard at Chatham in 1784. In 1797 the Admiralty was petitioned to take two carvers on to their strength at five dockyards. Although other dockyards complied with an order to this effect Chatham took another course and appointed George Williams as their "contract carver." Payments were now made through the Yard paybooks instead of direct from the Admiralty, an arrangement which ceased in 1813. The entries in the Chatham yard books were kept in great detail and show that between 1797 and 1813 George Williams carved 33 new figureheads, repaired 46 damaged figureheads, and restored damaged carved work on no less than 110 warships, including 20 captured Danish, Dutch and French vessels. Apart from the battles in which the ships were engaged there was also the storm damage which they suffered as they maintained the blockade of Brest in the face of Atlantic gales. Battle damage to the hulls of English warships was less than might be expected considering the tactics of the day of delivering broadsides at one's enemies at close range, but since the 1750's the French had concentrated on firing at the rigging and masts in order to cripple their opponents, not at the hull as did we. Chatham did not deal much with battle damage but after the Battle of Camperdown in October 1797 three 3rd. rates received his attention including the oddly named *Venerable*, a 3rd. rate 74 gun of 1784. *Monarch*, a 3rd. rate of 74 guns built in 1765 was repaired after the Battle of Copenhagen in April 1801. Another visitor to the yard was *Victorious*, a 3rd. rate of 74 guns, built in 1808 which defeated *Rivoli* in a single ship action in the Mediterranean in 1812.

He was also appointed by Sheerness as their carver but this yard only kept a record of the payments without any details. He was still being entered in the Sheerness books up to 1820. In 1802 Williams carved a new figurehead for *Victory* which had been built in Chatham in 1765 as a 1st. rate of 100 guns, and was being rebuilt at Chatham. For this he was paid £50, the cost of a single figure. He also carved a new taffrail for £36 and new quarters for £38, both prices below the 1737 allowance. A further £5.10.0. was spent on "two large eakings cut with scrowls terminating with pedestal and group of flowers." After the Battle of Trafalgar *Victory* was back at Chatham to have some battle damage repaired ;

Head repaired with Boys' Head, Legs, Arms, and part of the drapery, foliage etc.   £10. 0. 0
Upper finishing repaired in places   6. 0
A large bust of Lord Nelson for the taffrail. (a new feature)   5. 0. 0

In 1758 *Thames*, a 5th. rate of 32 guns was launched at Chatham, one of the last to be based on the same French design as *Unicorn* and *Lyme* built nearly sixty years earlier. George Williams was instructed to remove the figurehead of the captured French *Bourdelois*, repair it and fit it on the bows of *Thames*, a task for which he received £4.

Despite the Admiralty instruction of 1796 that only small repairs were to be carried out to damaged carved work, Chatham seems to have been given the go-ahead to undertake quite extensive renovation work. Take for example *Prince of Wales*, a 2nd. rate 90 guns built in 1794 which arrived at Chatham in 1810 for repairs:

"To George Williams, contract carver, in second quarter 1810, for repairs:
Two boy's arms and a leg
A goat's head and leg
Seven boys' wings
An eagle's head and three wings
A feather and crouch hand
Four roses for the cove
Four large arms with swords, branches, etc.
Two half arms with truncheons
A toe, scrawl, and piece of hair for the quarter. (scroll)
A unicorn's leg and lion's leg with scrowls (scrolls)
Fourteen feet of foliage like the old
Two arms with trumpets
Three arms with truncheons, etc. Four large brackets for the entry ports.   Total   £24. 1. 6"

In 1808 George Williams was commissioned to provide figureheads for two brigs building in a private yard in Newcastle for which he was paid through the Chatham pay books. A female bust for *Woodlark* of 16 guns and a male bust for the *Shearwater* of 10 guns, costing £3 each.

The Admiralty was prepared to disregard their own order of 1796 when it suited them. In 1812 they agreed to pay George Williams £75 for a figurehead for *Howe*, a 120 gun 1st. rate, under construction at Chatham and £113 for other carved work. By September the head was nearly ready, having been altered at the Navy's request and now costing £120 with extra carved work worth £74.8.0. More alterations were ordered and the cost of the figurehead soared to £220, having now become a bust of Earl Howe as a Roman senator with toga flung across the shoulder, with a 10'6" high figure on either side, one a sailor, the other a marine. The marine had originally had a firelock in his hand but this was changed so that his right hand touched his hat. This new price did not please the Admiralty who offered £105 for the finished job and not a penny more. Naturally George Williams was angry and wrote detailing the catalogue of changes which had taken him many weeks to carry out, but as no further letters have been found we do not know the result. Rest assured, Williams would be the loser.

From a letter which he wrote in 1834 begging for work it appears that he continued to carve for the yard at Chatham until 1832.

" Sirs,

I most humbly beg your pardon for troubling you but I am impel'd by necessity to state my case to you in the hope of relief. Yr. Hon'ble Board shortly after superannuating me on £24 a year, a sum too small to subsist on, gave me an order 9th. November 1832 for to do whatever carved work might be wanting in future in the Dockyard, Chatham to assist me which I have done until lately, (it now being done in Rotherhithe) and for want of which work I am in great distress, not being able to obtain the common necessities of life and support self and family by my utmost exertions. I beg to state that I have performed carved work at the Dockyard, Chatham ever since 9th. March 1784 and have ever given satisfaction to the respective officers under whom I have been employed. I now most humbly beg y'r Hon'ble Board will permit me to do whatever carved work is wanting there and I'll assure them, be the price what it may, that it can be done for, in a workmanlike manner by any person in Town or Rotherhithe, I will do it for the same price as I most earnestly wish to support myself and family the rest of my days." *(Public Record Office ADM 87/3, letter No. 255).*

Among the ships built at Chatham for which George Williams carved figureheads were *Revenge*, a 3rd. rate 74 guns of 1794, *Briton*, a 5th. rate 38 guns of 1812 and the 18 gun brig *Bacchus* of 1813, while from Sheerness came *Antelope*, a 4th. rate 50 guns of 1802 and *Mermaid*, a 5th. rate 32 guns of 1784.

Nehemiah Williams, London. In 1850 Nehemiah Williams wrote to the Admiralty and forwarded designs, models and estimates for a range of vessels.

Sirs, I have made bold to intrude myself to your notice as a competitor for the supply of ship carving requisite for Her Majesty's ships which work I am prepared to tender for (with your permission) at prices much below the present contract and will undertake by reference or specimens to ensure the best style that Art can produce." *(Public Record Office ADM 87/29, letter No. 4902).*

His first success was an order in 1850 for the carved work for *Brisk,* a sloop of 1,087 b.m., for which he received £5.0.0. The figurehead was critically examined by naval officers who were of the opinion that it was comparable with the carved work which the Navy received from other carvers. As a result of this favourable comment he was awarded a further order, this time for a figurehead for the 3rd. rate 80 gun screw vessel, *Brunswick* launched at Pembroke Dock in 1855 for which he was paid £25.18.0. He was also required to complete carved work for the stern and quarters. After it was completed in March 1850 it was kept until 1851 when it was sent to Pembroke Dock to be compared with the figurehead for *Hood* which had been carved by a member of the Hellyer family for this 2nd. rate 91 gun screw vessel which was eventually launched in 1859. The officers who examined the two figureheads reported that although the workmanship and appearance were good for both, they favoured *Hood's* figurehead.

From this time on the name of Nehemiah Williams appears only once more when he wrote to the Admiralty requesting again to be allowed to quote for carved work.

Joseph Wymhurst, Chatham. Wymhurst became carver for Chatham in 1700 and he at once became involved with the carvings for *Britannia,* a 1st. rate of 100 guns, assisting Matthias Fletcher. Wymhurst was paid £172.6.8 while Fletcher was paid £301.9.1. Shortly afterwards

Wymhurst took into partnership John Carter and Thomas Davidson and with them provided carved work for *Royal Sovereign,* another 100 gun 1st. rate. This time they were working alongside Joseph Helby and once more they received the smaller share of the payment, £1,623.16.0 for Helby and £26.17.4 for Wymhurst & Partners as they were now called. *Duke,* a 2nd. rate of 90 guns built in 1682 was stripped and rebuilt in 1701 when she was renamed *Prince George,* and the partnership was again helping Matthias Fletcher, but this time they did slightly better being paid £142.9.0 against Fletcher's £128.16.8.

Late in 1702 John Carter left the group only to rejoin in 1703. Thomas Davidson departed about the same time and set up on his own in Deptford. Carter quit again in 1704 leaving Wymhurst working on his own.

The War of the Spanish Succession began in 1702 and the yard was kept busy with repair work. The sums of money involved were generally small from *Triumph* of 1698, a 2nd. rate 90 guns, 12/-, to *Shrewsbury* of 1695, a 2nd. rate, 80 guns, £6.4.0. New carved work was provided for *Nightingale* a 6th. rate 24 guns built in 1702 for which they were paid £12.8.0, while for *Vigo,* a 4th. rate 48 guns of 1693, which was rebuilt after her recapture from the French in 1702, they cut new carvings worth £27.10.6. She was wrecked in 1703. He undertook repairs on seven of the warships which took part in the Battle of Vigo in October 1702, working on six of them in conjunction with Matthias Fletcher. The last bill submitted by Wymhurst was dated May 1706, but no details were recorded in the Accountant General's ledger.

5. Appendix
Main sources of information
Aberdeen City Archives. Alexander Hall & Co.

Business Records Dept., Glasgow University. Robert Duncan, Port Glasgow, Wm. Denny & Bros., Joseph Russell, Port Glasgow, Scott's of Greenock, Alex. Stephen & Sons, Glasgow, J. & G. Thomson/John Brown, Clydebank.

Dundee University. The papers of J. P. Ingram who carried out extensive research into Dundee shipping.

Lancaster Archives. John Brockbank of Lancaster. Matthew Simpson of Lancaster.

Liverpool Maritime Archives. Thos. & Jno. Brocklebank of Whitehaven.

Middlesbrough Archives. H. S. Edwards of South Shields.

National Maritime Museum. A. P. Elder's sketchbook, several old Shipwright's notebooks referring to carved work. Some early shipbuilding records.

Public Record Kew. ADM/20, The Accountant General's ledgers, 1661-1795, ADM/42, Yard Pay Books 1797-1815. ADM/87, Original letters between the dockyards and the Admiralty between 1832 and 1860, ADM/88, The index and precis of all the letters exchanged between 1832 and 1860, ADM/106, yard out letters from 1800 to 1830.

Alexander Turnbull Library, Wellington, New Zealand. Photograph collections. A. A. Boult, De Maus.

Scottish Record Office, Edinburgh. The bankruptcy proceedings against Scottish shipbuilders are indexed on the computer and these provide the names of carvers as creditors.

Strathclyde Regional Archives. Charles Connell, John Elder/Fairfield Ltd.

Victoria & Albert Museum. Anderson collection. Artist's sketchbooks ca. 1795 showing carved work.

Directory of Merchant Ship Carvers

In this list of names the dates given against each name represent those years in which there is a specific reference in an archive, a trades directory or a newspaper to a 'Ship Carver'. A carver probably worked outside those years quoted. The carvers are listed starting in London and going clockwise round the country. Where the name is in italics no further information has been found.

London Carvers.

John Anderson (d.ca. 1835)
R. Atkinson (Rotherhithe)	1829
R. Atkinson (Wapping)	1842-1844
Battin or Betton (London)	1768-
Batton & Glover (London)	-1799
William Browning (Rotherhithe)	1844
Henry Burnett (emigrated to U. S. A.)	ca.1750
Thomas Burrough (Deptford)	1743-1789
Henry Crouch emigrated to U. S. A.)	ca. 1760
Robert Williams Culmore (Rotherhithe)	1856-1875
Culmore & Long (Rotherhithe)	1875-1895
Charles Dark (Rotherhithe)	1833-1856
Alexander Pettigrew Elder (Limehouse and Blackwall) (b. 1828)	1853-1869
William Emery	1827-1829
George Faldo (b.1794) (Rotherhithe)	1808-1861
Robert Faldo (b.1826) (Rotherhithe)	1851-1887
David Gibb (Blackwall)	1878-1893 1900-1905
Gibb & Crichton (Blackwall)	1870-1877
John Grayfoot (Rotherhithe)	1801-1811
Grayfoot & Overton (Rotherhithe)	1812-1824
Grindling Gibbons	1600s
Robert Hall (Rotherhithe)	1832-1874
Messrs Hellyer	1810-1815
Hellyer & Browning (Rotherhithe)	1833-1842
Frederick Hellyer (Rotherhithe)	1844-1852
Thomas Hellyer (Blackwall)	1853-1872
Hellyer & Sons (Blackwall)	1873-1878
Hellyer & Co. (Blackwall)	1883-1902
John Henderson (Rotherhithe)	1829
J. Henderson (Rotherhithe)	1859-1861
Joseph Hodgson (Poplar)	1867-1883
Henry Hopkins (Rotherhithe)	1798-1824
John Hopkins (Rotherhithe)	1819
William Impey (Blackwall, Poplar)	1889-1894
Hiram Long (Rotherhithe)	1844-1872
Cornelius Luck (Blackwall)	1861-1888
Overton & Faldo (Rotherhithe)	1824-1829
Thomas Pritchard	1815
Thomas Smith (Limehouse)	1833-1844
Thomas Smith (Rotherhithe)	1844-1846
Henry White (Rotherhithe)	1800-1827
White & Williams (Rotherhithe)	1800
Nehemiah Williams (Rotherhithe)	1850-1856
Nehemiah Williams (d.1873) (Wapping)	1860-1873

105. *William Law's favourite subject was the eagle. This one was over the gates of the Eagle Mills in Dundee.*

South Coast Carvers
Robert Brown (Southampton)	1414
Richard Cowell (Southampton)	1883-1884
Edward Hellyer	1803-
J.E. & J. Hellyer (Cosham)	1861-1888
Otwell Jones (West Cowes)	1878
Albert Pearn (Polruan)	ca. 1897
Henry Trevenen (Plymouth)	1856-1876

In his book ' No Gallant Ship ' Michael Boquet states that an Italian craftsman lived in Plymouth and between about 1850 and 1860 he carved figureheads for Salcombe vessels such as *Zouave*.

Bristol Channel and Wales Carvers
John Robert Anderson (b. 1829).(Bristol)	1868-1914
Arthur Anderson (Bristol)	ca.1913
Williams & Anderson (Bristol)	1869
John Bailey (Bristol)	1830
William Bond (Bideford)	
Shon Edwards (Portmadoc)	ca. 1878
James M. Humberstone (Bristol)	1857
J. G. & A. Levison (Swansea)	1870-1897
Arthur Levison (Gloucester)	ca. 1910
Tom Owen (Appledore)	
Joseph Petherwick (Bideford)	1857
Joseph Pethybridge (Bristol)	1857
Rudd (Barnstaple)	1888-1903
Robert Price Williams (d. 1847).(Bristol)	ca.1815
Thomas Williams (Bristol)	1847-
Philip Witherstone (emigrated to U. S. A.)	1773

Liverpool Carvers
Andrew Allan	1846-1886
Allan & Co.	1852
Allan & Sons	1877-1880
Allan & Clotworthy	1857-1877
Thomas Allan	1880
Alexander Clotworthy	1860-1895
Hugh Clotworthy	1860-1877

William Dodd (d. ca 1921)	ca. 1850-
John Folds	1766-1799
John Folds jr.	1790-1799
George Hall	1846
Joseph Hammond	1837
John & Henry Hammond	1843-1846
John H. Hammond	1852-1869
Thomas Hammond	1860
John Hoar Hammond & Joseph Pim Hammond	1870-1895
John Hudson (Pt. St. Mary, I. O. M.)	
David Hughes	1867-1906
Innes & Edgar	1870
John Kenwright	1860-1886
R. Lee	
Hugh Logan	1843
Logan & Venn	1837-1839
William Rennie	1870
Archibald Robertson	1827-1859
A. & R. Robertson	1860
William Sayer	1843
J. & J. Usher	1843-1846
Ralph Usher	1832-1843
John Venn	1843-1857
James & John Venn	1857

North-East Coast Carvers.

John Askew (d. 1845).(Whitehaven.)	1807-1845
John Askew (d.1881). (Whitehaven)	1845-1881
George Brooker (b. 1824).(Workington)	-1881
James Brooker (b. 1816).(Maryport)	1842-1853
James Martin (Whitehaven / Maryport)	1869-1886
Henry Nutter (Whitehaven)	-1790
Ellis Nutter (1746-1809),(Whitehaven)	-1809
Thomas Richardson (Carlisle)	1858
Jonathan Shepherd (Whitehaven)	1855-1873
Keswick Wood (Maryport)	ca. 1838

Glasgow Carvers

M. & J. Allan (in name until 1900)	1839-1893
James Brooker (then to Sunderland)	1853-1854
John Crawford (b. 1849)	1875-1918
Charles Lizars Dobbie (b.1838)	1862-1903
William Drysdale	1889
Alexander Pettigrew Elder	1869-1882
W. & A. Houston	1855-1860
William Houston (b. 1820)	1860-1883
Andrew Hutton	1851-1860
Thomas Kay (d. 1852).(Dumbarton / Glasgow)	1834-1852
Kay & Shanks	1852-1857
Kay & Reid	1857-1889
T. Logan	1921-1926
Robert Lyness (b.1847)	1880-1883
Neil McLean	1842
Meiklejohn & Young	1859-1871
(Samuel Young b.1825)	
(George Meiklejohn b. 1834)	
Thomas Millar	1868-1871

William Nielson (b. 1822) Paisley.	1857-1882
A. & D. G. Reid	1881-1911
(Alexander Reid b.1834)	
(Douglas Reid b.1856)	
William Shanks	1848-1864
George Sutherland	1856-1864

Greenock and Port Glasgow Carvers.

James Allan, Jr.	1870-1885
Allan & Laurie	1851-1881
(Robert Robertson Laurie b.1830-d.1908)	
William Allan	1837-1842
John Buchan (b.1835-d.1910)	1859-1904
John Buchan (b.1859)	-1897
Henry Calder (b.1811)	1832-1841
William Calder (1792-d.1859)	1832-1841
Archibald Campbell (b.1789-d.1841)	1814-1841
Peter Christie (b.1806)	1834-1881
Peter Hay	1803
Josiah (Joseph) Humphries (b. 1831)	1873-1907
Thomas McCracken	1889-1900
Robert McGowan (b.1823-d.1869)	1847-1865
McMillan & Bathgate	1852-1915
(Hamilton McMillan and George Bathgate)	
Archibald McVicar	1821-1826
John Roberts (Port Glasgow)	1880-1920
Archibald Robertson	1821-1827
John Whitelaw	1886-1915

Moray Firth

Andrew Duncan (Garmouth)	late 1800's

Aberdeen Carvers

Charles Cook	1844
John Fraser	1869-1872
John Garvie	1885-1890
Gifford & Mair	1843
J. & J. Hay	1866-1886
William Hector	1883-1885
George Hellyer	1850-1852
George Hughes	1853-1889
Andrew McKay	1818-1836
James McKay	1834
Peter McMillan	1849-1851
Murray & Duguid	1865
J. Rutherford & Sons	1861-1893
(John Rutherford b.1839)	
John Smith (d.1892)	1824-1851
Alexander Wishart	1873-1874
James Wishart (b.1827)	1851-1881
George Wishart	1851-1854

Dundee Carvers

John Clark (Montrose)	1852-1867
Andrew Hutton (d.1851)	1845-1851
James Hutton (b.1832)	-1862
Andrew Hutton (b.1842)	-1862
James Law (b.1837-d.1903)	-1903
William Moyes Law (b.1852)	1872-1885

Alexander Leslie (d.1890)	1844-1867	**Sunderland Carvers**	
Quinn & McKenzie	1884	Benjamin Smith Bailes	1870-1879
Peter Quinn	1884-1885	Richard S. Branfoot	1850-1866
John Wynd (b.1799)	1840-1855	Branfoot & Swan	1850
		William Henry Bridges	1850-1869
Leith Carvers		James Brooker	1855-1859
Hugh Logan	1850-1861	William Brooker (b.1843)	1860-1863
Alexander Chalmers	1876	Bryson & Co.	1873
Alexander Sutherland	ca. 1835	Alexander Pettigrew Elder	1864-1868
		Sherarton Gowdy	1884
Newcastle Carvers		George D. Handy (b.1826)	1850-1890
William Allan (Jarrow)	1861-1862	Joseph Hodgson	1853-1856
John Anderson & Son	1821-1865	James Hutton	1865-1894
Thomas Anderson (b.1804).(S. Shields)	1845-1867	G.Kyle	1869
David Cockburn (S. Shields)	1855-1858	John G. Kyle	1888-1898
G. L. Davidson	1868	James Lindsay	1819-1827
William Doig	1851-1867	James Lindsay (b.1822)	1849-1882
Doig & Taylor	1858	John Lindsay (b.1794)	1834-1851
Richard Farrington	1778-1831	John Marshall	1836
Fisken ?	1870-1871	Joseph Melvin	1865-1888
Archibald & John Harriott (N. Shields)	1828-1840	George Pate	1839-1850
Archibald Harriott (N. Shields)	1840-1847	William Rutledge	1850-1866
Ralph Hedley	1869-1896	*Robert Smith*	1861-1880
Hellyer Bros. (S. Shields)	1867-1897	*William Smith*	1867-1897
William Hepburn	1850-1879	W. L. Snaith	1867-1896
Hepburn & Irwin	1875	George Tate	1843-1894
John Hudson. (N. Shields)	1854-1865	John Tate (b.1833), George Tate (b.1863)	
Francis Johnson	1847-1867	*Henry Wilson*	1827
John Johnson	1854-1865		
William Kyles	1844-1890	**Hull Carvers**	
Victor Mastaglio	1855-1881	*T. Catley*	1857-1863
George Millar	1861	*R. F. Hartley*	1857-1863
Adam Robertson	1837	*Henry Hartley*	1863
Robert Saddler Scott	1837-1844	J. Valentine Moloney	1848-1869
Peter Swan		*Richard Sansby*	1826-1837
James Taylor	1861-1865	*Robert Stevenson*	1863
J. D. Thompson (N. Shields)	1861-1879		

107. *Here is an example of another of the ship carvers' tasks, that of carving the decorative crest in the centre of the paddle boxes of the old steamers. The one in the photograph was taken from the paddle steamer* Caledonia *built in Port Glasgow in 1889 and preserved in the Wemyss Bay Pier buildings until it was removed to the Museum of Transport in Glasgow and restored. John Roberts was the carver for Reid's at this time.*

Directory of Carvers to the Naval Dockyards

Chatham

Thomas Fletcher	1660-1689
John Fletcher	1687-1693
Matthew (Matthias) Fletcher	1688-1713
Joseph Wymhurst	1700-1706
John Carter	1701-1704
Thomas Davidson	1701-1703
Richard Chichley	1713-1770
Abigail Chichley	1737-1743
Elizabeth Chichley	1764-1777
William Savage	1765-1783
George Williams	1784-1832
John Morley	1797

Deptford

John Fletcher	1659-1682
Joseph Helby	1679
	1694-1707
Matthew Fletcher	1690-1695
Richard Walker	1696
Thomas Davidson	1703-1715
Joseph Wade	1716-1743
Joseph Wade (junior)	1727-1740
Thomas Burrough	1743-1788
William Burrough	1790-1810
George Whitfield	1797-1815
Nathaniel Keast	1797-1815

Woolwich

Sebastian Vicars	1608-1610
Gerard Christmas	1615-1668
John Leadman	1659-1682
Joseph Helby	1679-1705
Matthew (Matthias) Fletcher	1685-1694
Robert Jones	1710-1721
Joseph Wade	1722-1743
Thomas Burrough	1743-1787
William Burrough	1790-1810

Kinsale

Ambrose Hunt	1696-1697
Henry Christmas	1696-1700
Abraham Hunt	1702-1703

Portsmouth

Samuel Ive	1660-1667
Robert Reynolds	1668-1669
Lewis Allen	1670-1705
Lewis Sawyer	1679
Thomas Coward	1696-1697
Robert Smith	1705-1724
William Smith	1724-1756
Cuthbert Mattingley	1756-1799
William Mattingley (son)	1773-1806
?? Jones (worked with Mattingley)	1778-1794
Hellyer & Co. (Also London and Shields)	1799-1899

Harwich

Gerard Christmas	1666-1668
Matthew (Matthias) Fletcher	1679

108. *The two pictures on this page show graphically how the Navy cut its carving costs over two hundred years. This is 'Ye King's Armes for ye Sterne.' Association, a 2nd. rate of 90 guns built in Portsmouth in 1697 was wrecked on the Scillies in 1707. The stern carving by Lewis Allen was preserved and years later was presented to the people of Penzance where it has been mounted in the Session Court. (Courtesy Penwith District Council.)*

Plymouth

John Pippin	1691
Anthony Allen	1691-1701
Thomas Allen	1696
Philip Reed	1701-1730
Maynard Nicholls	1735-1736
Cuthbert Mattingley	1737-1756
Thomas Pierce	1753-1770
Samuel Dickerson	1770-1790
James Dickerson	1790-1815
William Dickerson	1797-1815
Kinsman Pavey	1797-1820

Sheerness

Matthew (Matthias) Fletcher	1712
Richard Chichley	1713-1737
	1744-1768
Abigail Chichley	1737-1743
Elizabeth Chichley	1764-1777
William Savage	1765-1766
	1769-1783

Also under Naval Carvers

Robert Brown (Southampton)	1414
William Christmas (Blackwall)	1666
Richard Cord (Bristol)	1666
Frederick Dickerson (Plymouth)	1832-1860
Alexander Pettigrew Elder (London)	1856
George Faldo (London)	1832-1854
Grayfoot & Overton (London)	1815-1817
Robert Hall (London)	1832-1837
Richard Lawrence	1778
Thomas Pritchard	1815
Henry Trevenen (Plymouth)	1876

108. *After about 1830 only a floral 'drop' was permitted on the mullions between the windows on the stern, the number of 'drops' ranging from 8 on a 12 gun brig to 40 on a 100 gun 1st. rate. The cost went from 3/6 for small vessels to 5/- for large ones.*

Index of Merchant Ships

Italics indicate an illustration.

Index to Warships

111. *The Navy did not easily give up their desire to adorn their ships even after the introduction of the 'Ironclad'. They still carried an abundance of decorative work on the bow and stern. The sketches on this page and* page 112, *show the bow and stern carvings of the armoured cruiser* Galatea 5600/87, *built in Glasgow by Robert Napier. (Courtesy of Glasgow Museum of Transport. Redrawn by Richard Hunter).*

(See page 111 for caption.)

Index to Shipyards

References to shipyards are to be found in the text under the names of the carvers

Thomas Adamson, Dundee.
Andrew Hutton.

Thomas Alexander, Glasgow.
Neil McLean.

Alexander Anderson, Forres.
James Wishart.

William Anderson, Arbroath.
Andrew Hutton.

George Asplet, Jersey.
Nehemiah Williams.

Bally, Shoreham.
Nehemiah Williams.

Barclay & Robertson, Ardrossan.
M. & J. Allan.

William Barnard, Deptford.
Batton & Glover, John Grayfoot.

Barr & Shearer, Ardrossan.
Archibald Robertson.

Bartram & Sons, Sunderland.
Benjamin Smith Bailes, Richard S. Branfoot, G. L. Davidson, Joseph Melvin.

Black & Noble, Montrose.
C. L. Dobbie, Alexander Leslie.

Brockbank, Lancaster.
John Folds.

Thos. & Jno. Brocklebank, Whitehaven.
John Askew, James Brooker, Jonathan Shepherd.

Bronsdon & Wells, Deptford.
Thomas Burrough, Goddard.

John Brown & Co., Clydebank.
John Crawford.

Caird & Co., Greenock.
Allan & Laurie, Peter Christie.

J. & A. Calman, Dundee.
Andrew Hutton, Nehemiah Williams.

Campbell, Millar & Semple, Paisley.
William Nielson.

G. R. Clover, Liverpool.
Allan & Clotworthy.

Clyde S.B. & Eng. Co., Port Glasgow.
M. & J. Allan.

R. Cock & Sons, Bideford.
Mr. Rudd.

Colman & Martin, Dundee.
Andrew Hutton, James Hutton.

Charles Connell, Glasgow.
M. & J. Allan, Kay & Reid, A. & D. G. Reid.

Thomas Courthope, Rotherhithe
Richard Overton.

Cowan & Sloans, Ayr.
Logan & Venn.

Cumming & Ellis, Inverkeithing.
A. & D. G. Reid.

Cunliffe & Dunlop, Port Glasgow.
James Allen, jr.

William Denny, Dumbarton.
M. & J. Allan, Scott & Co., Greenock, Archibald Campbell, John Crawford, C. L. Dobbie, William Houston, Thomas Kay, Kay & Shanks, Kay & Reid, Robert C. Lyness, William Shanks, Archibald Robertson, George Sutherland.

Dobie & Co., Glasgow.
M. & J. Allan.

William Donald, Paisley.
Thomas Millar.

William Doxford & Sons, Sunderland.
Joseph Hodgson, James Lindsay, John Lindsay, William Rutledge.

Joseph Dudman, Deptford.
Grayfoot & Overton.

John Duncan, Kingston, nr. Elgin.
James Wishart.

Robert Duncan, jr., Port Glasgow.
Archibald Campbell.

Robert Duncan, Port Glasgow.
M. & J. Allan, James Allan jr., Kay & Reid, McMillan & Bathgate, John Roberts, John Whitelaw.

Dundee S. B. Co.
John Wynd.

H. S. Edwards, South Shields.
John Anderson, Richard Farrington, A. & J. Harriott.

John Elder & Co., Govan.
C. L. Dobbie, Kay & Reid.

Edward Esneuf, Jersey.
Nehemiah Williams.

Fairfield S. B. & Eng. Co., Govan.
John Crawford,

J. Fell, Workington.
Allan & Clotworthy.

Fellows & Co., Gt.Yarmouth.
Robert Hall.

D.& A. Fullerton, Ayr.
C. L. Dobbie, William Houston.

Gibson, McDonald & Arnold, Ramsay, Isle of Man.
George Sutherland.

Grangemouth Dockyard Co.
A. & D. G. Reid.

R. & H. Green, London.
Hellyer.

Alexander Hall, Aberdeen.
M. & J. Allan, Charles Cook, Charles Dark, John Fraser, J. & J. Hay, Hay & Lyall, William Hector, Hellyer, George Hughes, James Garvie, Robert Hall, Andrew McKay, James McKay, Peter McMillan, Murray & Duguid, John

Smith, James Wishart.

Hart & Stinnett, Liverpool.
Allan & Clotworthy.

K. Harvey, Littlehampton.
Nehemiah Williams.

R. & W. Hawthorn, Leslie.
Ralph Hedley.

Laurence Hill, Port Glasgow.
Kay & Reid.

A. & J. Inglis, Glasgow.
McMillan & Bathgate.

Jones & Quiggin, Liverpool.
Allan & Clotworthy.

Jordan, Liverpool.
Allan & Clotworthy.

Kirkpatrick & McIntyre, Port Glasgow.
M. & J. Allan.

James Laing, Sunderland.
Allan & Laurie, William Allen, Benjamin Smith Bailes, W. H. Bridges, James Brooker, William Brooker, Bryson & Co., A. P. Elder, Fisken, Ralph Hedley, Hellyer, Joseph Hodgson, J. G. Kyle, James Lindsay, Marshall, Joseph Melvin, George Pate, Robert Smith. W. L. Snaith, Nehemiah Williams, Wood Carving Co.

John Laird, Birkenhead.
David Hughes, Archibald Robertson.

Charles Lamport, Workington.
James Brooker,

Leckie, Wood & Munro, Torry.
George Hughes, James Wishart.

Liverpool Shipbuilding Co.
Allan & Clotworthy.

Lobnitz & Co., Renfrew.
Albert Works Co.

Lumley, Kennedy, Whitehaven.
James Brooker.

McCulloch & Patterson, Port Glasgow.
M. & J. Allan.

McFadyen & Co., Port Glasgow.
M. & J. Allan, James Allan, jr.

H. Mc Intyre, Alloa.
A. & D. G. Reid.

McKie & Thomson, Glasgow.
C. L. Dobbie.

A. McMillan & Son, Dumbarton.
William Houston.

James McMillan, Greenock.
Peter Christie.

J. McPherson, Perth.
William Law.

Marshall Bros., Shields.
Nehemiah Williams.

May & Thwaites of Shoreham.
Nehemiah Williams.

Charles Mitchell, Newcastle.
Ralph Hedley.

Muress & Clarke, Greenock.
William Calder.

James Napier, Glasgow.
   Kay & Reid, Andrew Hutton.
Robert Napier, Glasgow.
   Andrew Hutton, Kay & Reid.
Oswald, Mordaunt, Southampton.
   Dick Cowell.
Palmer Bros. & Co., Jarrow.
   Allan & Laurie.
William Parmetter, Gosport &
Southampton.
   Hellyer of Cosham.
Paterson, Bristol.
   Robert Price Williams.
Perth New Shipbuilding Company.
   James Law.
William Pile, Sunderland.
   John Lindsay.
William Pitcher, Northfleet.
   Robert Hall.
David Porter, Greenock.
   Archibald Campbell.
Frederick Preston, Great Yarmouth.
   Hellyer & Browning.
Ramage & Ferguson, Leith.
   Kay & Reid, David Gibb.
John Readhead & Sons, Ltd.,
Newcastle
   Hellyer, J. D. Thompson.
J. Reid & Co., Port Glasgow.
   James Allen, jr., John Roberts.
Richardson Bros., Stockton.
   M. & J. Allan.
Ritson & Co., Whitehaven.
   James Brooker.
Francis Robertson, Peterhead.
   George Hughes.
Robinson & Russell, Millwall.
   Hellyer.
A. Rodger & Co., Port Glasgow.
   John Roberts.
Roy & Mitchell, Alloa.
   Alexander Leslie.
T. Royden & Co., Liverpool.
   Archibald Robertson.
Russell & Co., Port Glasgow.
   British Charrier Carving Co., John

Buchan, John Crawford, Joseph
Humphries, Robert C. Lyness,
McMillan & Bathgate, John Roberts.
Scotswood S.B.Co.
   Ralph Hedley.
J. E. Scott, Greenock.
   McMillan & Bathgate.
Scott's Shipbuilding & Engineering
Co., Greenock.
   James Allan jr., Allan & Laurie,
   British Charrier Carving Co. Peter
   Christie, John Crawford, C. L. Dobbie,
   Henry Hopkins, Joseph Humphries,
   Thomas McCracken, McMillan &
   Bathgate, John Roberts, Archibald
   Robertson, John Whitelaw.
Scott & Linton, Dumbarton.
   Hellyer.
John Scott & Sons, Greenock.
   Archibald McVicar.
John Scott & Sons, Inverkeithing.
   Alexander Chalmers, Thomas Dunn.
John Scott & Co., Kinghorn.
   A. & D. G. Reid.
Scott & Sons, Bowling.
   R.Mc Gowan.
A. Shearer, Glasgow.
   McMillan & Bathgate.
Short, Bros., Sunderland
   George D. Handy, David Hughes,
   James Hutton, James Lindsay, Joseph
   Melvin.
M. Simpson, Lancaster.
   Logan & Venn.
J. Slade, & Sons, Polruan.
   Albert Pearn.
David Smeaton, Perth.
   James Law.
John Smith, Aberdeen.
   James Walker, James Wishart.
R. Smith, Preston.
   Allan & Clotworthy.
Robert Steele, Greenock.
   Archibald Robertson.
Alexander Stephen, Dundee.
   James Hutton, James Law.
Alexander Stephen, Linthouse.

M. & J. Allan, John Crawford,
   C.L.Dobbie, Andrew Hutton, T. Logan.
Robert Stewart, Inverness.
   Joseph Melvin.
Henry Sutton, Leith.
   M. & J. Allan.
Swan, Hunter, Newcastle.
   Ralph Hedley.
Benjamin Tanner, Dartmouth.
   Henry Hopkins.
J. & G. Thomson, Clydebank.
   M. & J. Allan, John Crawford, C. L.
   Dobbie,William Houston, Andrew
   Hutton, R. McGowan, Archibald
   Robertson.
Thomson & Spiers, Greenock &
Troon.
   William Allen, William Calder, Neil
   McLean, Peter Christie.
Union Shipbuilding Co., Glasgow.
   Kay & Reid.
Thomas Vernon, Liverpool.
   Allan & Clotworthy, James Brooker,
   William Dodd.
James Warwick, Rotherhithe
   Henry White.
John Watson, Banff.
   Nehemiah Williams.
J. Samuel White, Cosham.
   Hellyer.
Joseph White, Cowes, Isle of Wight.
   Robert Hall.
Thomas White, (The Younger),
Portsmouth.
   Robert Hall.
Whitehaven Shipbuilding Co.
   James Brooker.
Wigham, Richardson, Newcastle.
   Ralph Hedley.
Wigram & Green, London.
   George Faldo.
Charles Wood, Port Glasgow.
   Peter Christie.
James Wood, Port Glasgow.
   Archibald Roberston.
Keswick Wood, Maryport.
   James Brooker, Mr. Keswick Wood.

Errata
P.36. The first line is repeated from P.35 and should be ignored.
P.44. **Kay & Reid,** line 3 should read "from 5 men and 5 boys in 1861 to 35 men and 19 boys by 1871."
P.52. **Neil Mclean,** This paragraph is incomplete and should continue : " *Janet Wilson 280/43* which they were building and was paid £3.0.0 for his efforts. McLean also cut work for Thomas Alexander of Glasgow who went bankrupt in 1842 owing him £8.4.0, while they were completing the brig *Caribbean 83/421*
Additional material uncovered after printing had commenced.
Allan & Clotworthy. Allan & Clotworthy held 12 shares in the Liverpool Shipbuilding Company which lasted only four years from 1867 to 1871. Presumably they hoped that as shareholders they would be given preference over other carvers.
Richard Overton   In 1824 Overton carried out work on a number of East Indiamen at the shipyard of Thomas Courthope of Rotherhithe. They included *Warren Hastings 997/08* and *Earl of Balcarras 1417/15*.
Henry Hopkins. In 1802 Henry Hopkins repaired the figurehead, stern and quarters of the brig *Anna Bella*.

Naval Lion of the 18th Century.